Praise for Paul Ferrini's Books

The most important book I have read. I study it like a bible!" Elisabeth Kubler-Ross, M.D., author of *On Death and Dying.*

"These words embody tolerance, universality, love and compassion—hallmarks of all Great Teachings. They turn our attention inward to our own divine nature, instead of diverting it outward. Paul Ferrini is a modern-day Kahlil Gibran—poet, mystic, visionary, teller of truth." Larry Dossey, MD., author of *Healing Words: The Power of Prayer and the Practice of Medicine.*

"Paul Ferrini leads us skillfully and courageously beyond shame, blame and attachment to our wounds into the depths of self-forgiveness. His work is a must-read for all people who are ready to take responsibility for their own healing." John Bradshaw, author of *Family Secrets.*

"A breath of fresh air in an often musty and cluttered domain. With sweetness, clarity, and simplicity we are directed to the truth within. I read this book whenever my heart directs, which is often." Pat Rodegast, author of *Emmanuel's Book I, II and III.*

"Paul Ferrini's writing is authentic, delightful and wise. It reconnects the reader to the Spirit Within, to that place where even our deepest wounds can be healed." Joan Borysenko, Ph.D., author of *Guilt is the Teacher, Love is the Answer.*

"I feel that this work comes from a continuous friendship with the deepest part of the Self. I trust its wisdom." Coleman Barks, poet and translator.

"Paul Ferrini's wonderful books show a way to walk lightly with joy on planet earth." Gerald Jampolsky, M.D., author of *Love is Letting Go of Fear.*

"Paul Ferrini leads us on a gentle journey to our true source of joy and happiness—inside ourselves." Ken Keyes, Jr., author of *The Handbook of Higher Consciousness.*

Book Design by Paul Ferrini and Elizabeth Lewis
Typesetting by Kay Yamaguchi

Photograph on page 6 by Mark Caryl.
Photograph on back cover and page 14 of painting by Heinrich
Hoffman through Self-Realization Fellowship.
Photograph on front cover and on page 176 by Barbara McAlley
through Carol Bruce and Robert Ferre.

ISBN #1-879159-15-5

Manufactured in the United States of America

Love Without Conditions
Reflections of
the Christ Mind

by Paul Ferrini

Table of Contents

Author's Preface

With all of the fanfare about channeling, it seems important to be clear that this is not a channeled book. The information in this book does not come from some "entity" or personality apart from the mind of the listener. Indeed, this book is the result of one listener's joining with the Christ Mind, of which he and you are essential parts.

To think of Jesus as being outside of and independent of your mind is to miss the point. For it is in your mind that Jesus addresses you. He is your most intimate friend speaking to you, sometimes in words, often beyond words. Your communication and communion with him is essential to your practice of his teaching.

Let us be clear that Jesus has no exclusive place or position in the Christ Mind. Krishna, Buddha, Moses, Mohammed, Lao Tzu, and many others are consciously joined with him there, or perhaps I should more accurately say "here." If you feel more comfortable addressing yourself to Buddha or Krishna, please do so. Jesus will not be offended. Indeed, he will be pleased, because you are following his teaching of non-separation.

We all commune and communicate with the Christ Mind (you can say Buddha Mind or Brahman or Holy Spirit if you prefer). That is because we are all joined with the Mind of God. If this were not true, our experience would be totally dark and without even the promise of redemption.

Each of us has a tiny spark of light that illuminates the darkness of our unconsciousness. This is the divine spark of awareness which keeps our connection with God alive. This spark also connects us to the divine teacher in our tradition and to the divinity within our brothers and sisters.

As Jesus points out in this book, were we to see only that spark of light within each one of us, all darkness in our perception and experience would dissolve, and the world as we know it would disappear. This is how love is established in our own heart and in the hearts of our brothers and sisters.

Do not make the mistake of thinking that any reflection of the Christ Mind seeks anything other than the establishment of the kingdom of love in our minds and hearts. That is its single goal. Mahavir works for this. St. Francis works for this. The Baal Shem Tov works for this. Rumi works for this.

Divisions into religions are relics of this world. Such boundaries do not exist in the Christ Mind, where all beings join in a single goal. It is hard for us to imagine this, but it is so.

There is no one brought up in the Judeo— Christian tradition who does not have to come to terms with the life and teachings of Jesus. This is true for Christians and Jews alike. It is also true for atheists or agnostics.

Jews need to understand and accept the transmission of faith Jesus brought to them. Christians need to understand how his teachings of love and forgiveness have been inverted into teachings of fear and guilt. Atheists need to understand his revolutionary message of equality.

All who have rejected Jesus or placed him on a pedestal have misunderstood his teaching. That is why correction must take place for all of us. To each one of us, Jesus has a specific message that will help us dissolve our guilt and walk through our fear.

Jesus does not ask us to convert to Christianity, for there is no such thing. Christianity is a myth of separation. It divides the Christian from the Jew or the Muslim or the Buddhist. Do you think Jesus would advocate such an idea?

Of course not!

A follower of Jesus does not advocate any kind of separation. He practices love and forgiveness for all beings, including himself. He embraces the Jew, the Muslim and the Hindu as his brother. He does not seek to convert others, but rests secure in his own faith. Nor does he believe that those who choose a different path will be denied salvation. A true follower of Jesus knows that God has many ways of bringing us home and never doubts the outcome.

Each of us has available to us a personal

relationship with Jesus. That relationship comes into being simply as we begin to want it and trust it. There is no technology, no invocation, no esoteric spiritual practice involved in it. The simple but authentic need for his friendship and his guidance is all that is required.

Let's be clear that Jesus does not wish to become an authority figure for us. Indeed, he stands against all authority save God's. He asks merely that we take his hand as an equal, and that we reach out to each one of our brothers and sisters with the same mutual respect and intention of equality.

His teaching may be simple, but it will require all of our attention, all of our energy, all of our commitment to put it into practice. To intend to "be equal with" each person in our experience, and to recognize and forgive all mistakes as they happen is a revolutionary teaching. It is a teaching that will wash away our guilt away and help us move through our fears.

When I began to work on this project, I brought to it the same degree of surrender which I had brought to previous books. That however, was not enough. In quiet recognition I put aside approximately 150 pages of good material. It simply wasn't the book that needed to be birthed at this time in my life. Something new was being asked of me. And I was asking something new of my teacher.

I wanted a simple, lucid book that would help clarify our relationship with Jesus and with his teaching. And as I asked, it became clear that, to write such a book, something of Paul needed to move aside. Paul's identity needed to be challenged. His belief systems, his vocabulary, needed to be loosened up. Ideas that made him feel separate from others needed to be dynamited away. Unless these things happened, the book could not come through.

During this process, I learned to rely more on my relationship with Jesus than on anything I had read by or about him. I also saw Jesus diligently working in the lives of many people who seemed to hold beliefs that differed from my own.

Beliefs separate. Loving thoughts unite. "If you want to follow my teaching, live it thought by thought. Bless your brother, even though you don't agree with him." This had always been Jesus' teaching. Now, he was just taking it into a wider arena.

Letting this book come from Jesus and the Christ Mind meant making an adjustment in all areas of my life. It required not so much a change in my writing style or process, but a fundamental shift in my belief systems. Removing the "ideas that give rise to perceptions and feelings of separation" had to become my daily spiritual practice.

I assure you that I have been anything but perfect in this practice. But I feel profoundly grateful for the practice and for this book, because both have helped me to take a very difficult step forward in my spiritual growth.

It is my hope that this book will extend to you

a simple but profound practice of self-forgiveness and non-separation that will transform your life. This is the practice that Jesus perfected in his life here. And it is the practice that he continues to advocate moment to moment as we reach out and ask for his help in our lives.

Ultimately, the end of human suffering comes when we decide together that we have suffered enough. Each of us, in our own lives, is beginning to ask for a better way. Do you think that Jesus will abandon us now? Do you think the little spark in your heart and mine will shrink and grow dim, a casualty of our fear, our guilt, and our pain?

It cannot be so.

The love of Jesus, Krishna, Buddha, and all the ascended masters surrounds us in our single prayer. It gently nurtures the spark in our hearts, helping us move more completely through our fear and shame. It brings divine illumination to all the narrow beliefs and conditions of our experience.

Because the light is within us, it cannot refuse to shine when we call upon it. The light of Christ is within us all. Let us invoke it together, in the name of love.

Paul Ferrini
Santa Fe, New Mexico
December, 1993

Introduction

et me begin by saying that I speak through you only to the extent that you are willing to relinquish control. In that sense, you are not special. I can speak through anyone who has that willingness.

What you hear has a great deal to do with what is already present in your mind. Each person who opens to my voice will hear it according to his own perceptions and preconceptions. That is inevitable.

The desire to communicate with me is essential to opening the door to my presence. I will not force myself upon anyone. The relationship with me is voluntary and must be initiated by each person when he is ready.

I am as close to you as you would have me be. That is because I am already a thought within your mind. And everything that I am proceeds from that thought, just as everything which is not me proceeds from a different thought. This you must learn through experience.

Some claim that I speak through them, yet they are listening to a different voice. My voice never condemns or makes fearful. My intention is to bless everyone. I would have each of you know once and for all that you are not guilty except in your own mind, and that imagined guilt can and must be undone.

My teaching is a simple one: I teach the forgiveness of sins. I teach that sin itself is not real. It seems to be real only because you believe that you can be injured. You believe that you are the body, and so when the body has been injured, you believe that an injustice has been done to you.

I understand that it is hard for you to relinquish that belief. Yet that is what I ask you to do. You are not the body, for the body is born and dies, and you are not born, nor do you die.

You are no thought of limitation, for every thought that limits you is a body that will begin and end. The body is just the scope of your beliefs. There are dense bodies and light bodies, but all have a beginning or end. All are subject to some form of self conscription.

I am a thought without limitation, for I am ever expanding into the formlessness of God. There is no form that can contain me. I have joined with God in perfect forgiveness. I am free of guilt. I am free of grievances. I do not believe that I can be wronged, nor do I believe that I have the power to wrong another. For I know without a doubt that every being has equality in God.

I know that it is hard for you to believe this, for so much that you see in your world suggests inequity. But these inequities are simply of your own making. They are an untruth that you sustain.

You need sustain them no longer. Demonstrate that they are not real by extending the love of God to every one of your brothers. Only in this way can the kingdom of God be experienced on earth.

Do not concern yourself with what others do or leave undone. It is not your responsibility to evaluate their thoughts or their actions. Simply be responsible for how you think and act. For if you think and act with God you will influence others without saying a single word.

Charity is found only in self-responsibility. Do the very best that you can do for yourself and others and leave the rest for God to do.

You are not responsible for the choices that others make, nor are they responsible for yours. However, you can and must learn from one another, for what you choose is not that different from the choice your brother makes. You make many of the same mistakes.

Mistakes are opportunities for learning. To condemn your brother for making mistakes is to pretend to be mistake free, which you are not. I have asked you before and I will ask you again: which one of you will throw the first stone?

You can release your brother from the judgment you would make of him within your own mind. To release him is to love him, for it places him where love alone lies, beyond judgment of any kind.

Mastery of your own thoughts is essential for

your enlightenment. For it is in your thoughts that you choose to walk with me or to walk away from me.

I am constant, unlike you. I will not walk away from you. I stand always at your side, waiting for you to acknowledge me.

If you would be like me you must learn to think like me. And if you would learn to think like me you must place every thought you think in my hands. I will tell you if it is helpful or not. Unhelpful thoughts must be eliminated. That is the essence of mind training. Only thoughts that bless and recall us to truth shall be retained.

My teaching has been and will continue to be distorted because it threatens every thought which is false. And so threatened, false thoughts take hold of the teaching and seek to mold it to fit their ends. It does not take long before the words attributed to me are the opposite of the ones that I have said.

This is why I ask you to be vigilant. Do not resist this distortion, attack it or seek to discredit it, for that will just make it stronger. But be clear in your own mind and reject the false for the sake of truth.

A single false idea can bring the mind that thinks it to despair. But a single true thought restores the kingdom. Therefore, choose your thoughts wisely. And if you are uncertain what to think, bring your dilemma to me.

Surrendering to me is unlike any act of surrender you can know in the world. For the world would use your surrender harshly to control you, but I would use it gently to release you from falsehood and give you back your true Self.

Those who do my work empower you to love and affirm yourself as you are right now. Those who work against me find many faults with you, which they would fix. They would make you dependent on them for your salvation. Do not accept such lies. Learn to discriminate. No one on earth has a better answer for you than the one you will find through trust in yourself and in me.

The Core Issue

There is no one else who is as hard on yourself as you are. Like all your brothers and sisters, you suffer from a basic sense of inadequacy and unworthiness. You feel that you have made terrible mistakes which will sooner or later be punished by humans in authority or by some abstract spiritual authority like God, or karmic law.

These unresolved issues of self-worth are the conditions of your embodiment. In other words, you are here to work them out. You selected your parents to exacerbate your guilt so that you could become conscious of it. Thus, blaming them for your problems will not help you remove the conditions you have mutually placed on love. The only way out is through your expanding awareness of your own guilt and fear-based beliefs and patterns of interaction.

Seeking someone special to provide the love your parents weren't able to provide will not help either. It just raises the temperature in the pressure cooker. Don't be surprised if the mate you choose is the perfect embodiment of the parent with whom you most need to heal. You cannot but come face to face with your own wounds. Parents, spouses and children are here to help you see your own need for healing, and you are performing the same function in their lives.

Looking for unconditional love in a world of conditions must inevitably fail. Since all your brothers and sisters are acting out of shame-based patterns, they cannot offer you the love you know that you deserve, nor can you offer it to them. The best that you can do is raise each other's awareness of the love that is necessary and begin taking responsibility for giving it to yourself.

If you do not take responsibility for bringing love to your own wounds, you will not move out of the vicious cycle of attack/defense, guilt and blame. Your feelings of rage, hurt and betrayal, all of which seem justified, will just fuel the fire of interpersonal conflict and continue to reinforce your unconscious belief that you are unlovable and incapable of loving.

You must learn to see the extent of your own self-hatred. Until you look in the mirror and see your own beliefs reflected there, you will be using every brother or sister in your experience as a mirror to show you what you believe about yourself. While there is nothing wrong with this practice, it is not the shortest or the easiest way home, since there is always the tendency to think that what you see is somebody else's lesson.

If you want to step outside the vicious psychology of the world, you must stop the game of projection.

This game hides your unconscious death urge behind a facade of blame and conditional morality. It is ironic, indeed, but at the very instant at which you are proclaiming your innocence at your brother's expense, you are also reinforcing your own feelings of guilt and inferiority.

There is no way out of the circle of blame but to stop blaming. Yet, be prepared. If you would step off the wheel of suffering, you may find that you aren't very popular. Those who don't join in the world's game of projection are the very first to be attacked. If you learned nothing from my life, you must have learned this!

Anyone who would acknowledge his own fear without projecting it threatens the world's game. Anyone who would own his murderous thoughts and seek to find their roots within consciousness threatens the moral fabric of society.

In human society there is a right and a wrong. Those who do right are rewarded and those who do wrong are punished. This is how it has always been.

My teaching threatens this basic assumption. At the most superficial level it challenges the idea that wrongs should be punished. In the face of the call for retribution, I have stood and will continue to stand for forgiveness.

At a deeper level my teaching challenges the very idea that someone should be condemned by his behavior. If someone acts wrongly, it is because he thinks thoughts that are false. If he can realize the untruth of his thinking, he can change his behavior. And it is in the interest of society to help him do this. But if punishment is brought, his false ideas will be reinforced, and guilt will be added to them.

You have heard the expression "two wrongs do not make a right." That is the essence of my teaching. All wrongs must be corrected in the right manner. Otherwise correction is attack.

To oppose, seek to overpower or argue with a false idea is to strengthen it. That is the way of violence. My way, on the other hand, is nonviolent. It demonstrates the answer in its approach to the problem. It brings love, not attack, to the ones in pain. Its means are consistent with its ends.

To make wrong is to teach guilt, and perpetuate the belief that pain and suffering are necessary. To make right is to teach love and demonstrate its power to overcome all suffering. To put it simply, you are never right to make wrong, or wrong to make right. To be right, make right.

You cannot love in an unloving way. You can't be right and attack what's wrong. Error must be undone. And since the root of all error is fear, only the undoing of fear will bring correction.

Love is the only response that undoes fear. If you don't believe this, try it. Love any person or situation that evokes fear in you and the fear will disappear. This is true, not so much because love is an antidote to fear, but because fear is "the absence of love." It therefore cannot exist whenever love is present.

Most of you understand a great deal about fear, but very little about love. You are afraid of God, afraid of me, and afraid of one another.

Why are you afraid? Because you believe that you are neither lovable nor capable of loving another.

That belief is the only belief that needs to be changed. All negativity in your life will fall away as you undo this simple erroneous belief about yourself.

You, my friend, are not what you think you are. You are not simply an accumulation of all your negative beliefs and actions. That is who you think you are, but that is not who you are.

You are God's son, even as I am. All that is good and true about God is good and true about you. Accept this fact, even for an instant, and your life would be transformed. Accept this about your brother, even in this single moment, and all conflict between you would end.

What you see is a direct result of what you believe. If you believe that you are guilty, then you will see a guilty world. And a guilty world will be punished and so will you.

"God will bring you down. God will destroy the world. God will have His revenge." These, my friends, are the thoughts that you think. These — blasphemous though they be — are the absurd ideas you would attribute to me! Fortunately, I understand that this is just your not so subtle way of beating yourself up.

It is a delaying maneuver. In time, you will

tire of it. It will not be long before you begin to reject the whole concept of guilt — individually and collectively — and aspire to come home.

My friends, I await that moment of complete honesty and responsibility with joy and certainty. On that day, when you see your good and that of your brother as one and the same, all that separates you from God will fall away and you will stand beside me in all your splendor.

Then you will know God's love for you beyond any doubt. Then you will know that She never abandoned you, even in the height of your insanity when you thought it was She who would punish you and destroy your world. Then you will know the power of your mind to create, and then will you choose to create with God, not apart from Her.

Practice

The very word practice invites misunderstanding. What would you practice except that which you already know? And what do you know except guilt, fear and attack? Certainly you do not want to continue to practice the very beliefs and reactions which lead to your suffering!

So what shall you practice? Perhaps you could begin by simply practicing awareness. Practice being aware of your guilt, your fear and your attack. Do not disguise them, deny them, or project them onto other people. Merely look at these phenomena as they arise within your consciousness.

When you feel angry or depressed, simply ask "Why am I angry? Why am I feeling the need to defend myself? What am I afraid of? Continue to ask these questions until you begin to see the source of your anger and fear. Once you get through these layers of emotion, ask yourself "what is my guilt here?"

What guilt you ask? All negative emotions in your life arise from your unconscious guilt/shame. This must become conscious. It must be brought into your awareness so that you can release it.

Your feelings of inadequacy and unworthiness create your fear of retribution. If you believe that there is something wrong with you or that you have done something wrong, you will be afraid of being punished. And if you are afraid of being punished, you will defend yourself against all imagined attack. Whenever you feel that someone is questioning your self worth, you will be ready to pull the trigger.

This whole scene of guilt and retribution is happening only in your own mind. If you project it, you will bring others into it and you will need to work it out together. This just ups the ante. Working something out with another when you are not aware of your own complicity in the event is unlikely.

Better to begin by bringing an awareness to your own thoughts. For not only will you find that guilt is the root of all suffering, you will also find that self-forgiveness is necessary. Without self-forgiveness, there is no release from guilt. So the drama of redemption is also happening only in your own mind.

In your mind, you establish your innocence or guilt. It does not matter how many people abused you. Blaming them will not help you. You are the judge who pronounces sentence. And so long as you are blaming someone else for your problems, you are refusing to offer forgiveness to yourself.

Judge and jury live within your own thoughts. You established your guilt and now you must dissolve it. Until you undo your guilt, you cannot find your innocence. That is what the forgiveness process is all about. It has nothing to do with forgiving others. It has everything to do with forgiving yourself for establishing your guilt.

This is the realm of practice. There is no situation where this work cannot be undertaken. The whole scenario of your life is territory for self-inquiry. Bring your awareness to every thought and every feeling and you will soon find the source of your guilt and your subsequent suffering.

No one can escape this work. It is an essential part of the curriculum of awakening. The sooner you realize it, the easier it will be for you.

Your Brother

You are constantly overestimating your brother's importance in your life. On the one hand, you would like to blame him for all of your problems, and crucify him, as you did me. And on the other hand, you would like to raise him onto a pedestal and worship him, as you worship me.

You have a very hard time, however, treating your brother as an equal. When I asked you to love your neighbor as yourself, I gave you a very simple rule to go by in your affairs. Unfortunately, if you do not love yourself, you won't have much luck loving your neighbor.

Learning to love yourself and learning to love your brother go hand in hand. You can't love your brother and hate yourself, or love yourself and hate your brother. Your feelings about your brother simply mirror your feelings about yourself.

As such, your interactions with your brother help you to see what you must forgive in yourself. Forgiving your brother for his trespass on you only helps him if it enables him to forgive himself. Likewise, receiving your brother's forgiveness for your trespass on him only helps you if it enables you to forgive yourself.

The forgiveness of others is necessary only if you believe that it is. If you do, as most people do, making amends is important. Asking others for forgiveness demonstrates that you are ready to change your own mind about what happened. That is an important first step in the process.

However, do not make the mistake of giving your brother the "power" to forgive you. This places power outside of yourself, where it can never be. Ask for his forgiveness but, if he withholds it, do not assume that forgiveness will never be yours. Indeed, it is always yours. Those who withhold forgiveness only withhold it from themselves.

If you find yourself condemning your brother, you can be sure that it is not him you condemn. It is some shamed part of yourself you have not acknowledged. Perceiving inadequacy in your brother cannot make you feel better, for it merely aggravates your own sense of unworthiness.

Neither justice nor salvation are to be gained by attacking your brother. Please see this for what it is. Every nail you pound into your brother's hand holds you to the cross. I am the proof of that. For I will remain on the cross in your perception until all attack stops. Until then, you and I share something in common: we have both been crucified.

In your interactions with your brother, you have a simple choice: to find him innocent or to find him guilty. This choice occurs over and over again, every day, every hour, every moment. Thought by thought, you imprison your brother or release him. And as you choose to treat him, so do you deliver the same judgment upon yourself.

You cannot get to heaven by holding your brother down, nor will you get there if you try to carry him. Each of you has been given the means to discover your own innocence. Simply acknowledge your brother and bless him upon his journey. If he asks for your help, give it gladly. But do not try to do for your brother what he must do for himself.

Proper boundaries are necessary if you are to move beyond them. Don't make your peace and happiness your brother's responsibility, or make his peace and happiness yours. He is not here to save you, nor you to save him.

On the other hand, release your brother from every grievance you have of him. Do not withhold love from him in any way. For to try to hold him back from his happiness is but to attack him and imprison yourself in the grip of fear and guilt.

Do not avoid your brother's call for help. Let him work by your side as long as he will. And when he is ready to leave, wish him well. Give him food and water for the journey. Don't make him beholden to you or force him to stay against his will.

Your brother's freedom is but a symbol for your own. Therefore, let him come and go gracefully. Welcome him when he comes and bid him farewell when he goes. More than that you cannot do. Yet this much is enough. Care for each stranger in this way, and I will show you a world where trust has returned and charity rules.

Love your neighbor as you would love yourself. Make him equally important. Do not sacrifice for him or ask him to sacrifice for you, but help him when you can and receive his help gratefully when you need it. This simple dignified exchange is a gesture of love and acceptance. It demonstrates mutual confidence and mutual regard.

More than this is too much. Less than this is too little.

Interpretation

You interpret what happens in your life according to your core beliefs and the emotional states that arise from them. The experience of disappointment, for example, relates directly to your guilt and feelings of inadequacy.

When your expectations are not met, you are merely receiving a correction. You are being told that you do not see the whole truth of a situation. You are being asked to expand your perceptions. Correction is not attack. It is not punishment.

The perception that you are being attacked or punished when things do not go your way is entirely guilt-driven. Without that guilt, the correction would be received with gratitude, and perception would be expanded to include the new information.

All experience happens for one purpose only: to expand your awareness. Any other meaning you see in your life experience is a meaning that you made up. You may not decide at a conscious level what will happen to you, but you most definitely interpret what happens according to your beliefs.

Your primary freedom lies in accepting and learning from the experiences that come your way.

Of course, you can reject your experience. You can refuse to learn from it. But this choice leads to suffering. If you don't know this yet, it won't be long before you do.

You might ask: "can I remove suffering by accepting my experience and learning from it?" That is a very good question. Not only can you remove suffering, you can experience the joy of union with God. For in the embrace of your experience, correction is received and your thoughts are brought into alignment with the Divine Mind.

Life is either resistance or surrender. These are the only choices. Resistance leads to suffering. Surrender leads to bliss. Resistance is the decision to act alone. Surrender is the decision to act with God.

You cannot experience joy in life by opposing the ideas or actions of other people. You can experience joy only by remaining faithful to the truth within your own heart. And this truth never rejects others, but invites them in.

Truth is a door that remains open. You cannot close this door. You can choose not to enter. You can walk in the opposite direction. But you can never say: "I tried to enter, but the door was closed." The door is never closed to you or anyone else.

If you feel that the door has been shut in your face, you have interpreted your experience in a fearful way. You believe the door is shut. It isn't, but your belief that the door is shut may very well convince you and others that this is the case.

You are all masters at taking truth and inverting it. You have the creative ability to make anything mean what you want it to mean. You can take yes and make it no, wrong and make it right. That is how strong your beliefs are.

But just because you have inverted truth does not mean the truth ceases to be true. It means only that you have succeeded in hiding the truth from yourself.

So how you interpret your experience is rather important. When your expectations are frustrated, will you accept the correction or will you insist that you are being unfairly treated? Are you the victim of what happens to you, or the one who uses it for learning? Are you receiving your experience as a blessing or as a punishment? That is the question you must constantly ask yourself.

Every experience is an opportunity to embrace truth and reject illusion. One experience is not better or worse than another in this respect. All experiences are equally potent. They exist only as a birthing ground for your divinity.

That is why you must never despair. You will always have another chance to change your mind. Don't listen to those who would tell you otherwise. There is no final judgment, except for the judgment you will make about yourself when you see yourself through my eyes.

Perhaps in this moment you do not believe me. Perhaps you are convinced that you have caused the suffering of others or that you are the victim of their actions toward you. Just because you reject my words now does not mean that I will cease to offer them to you. Why should it matter to me how long it takes for you to wake up?

Certainly, time is not an issue for me. Nor is it for you, if truth were told. You have plenty of time to make mistakes and learn from them.

When every one of you has learned what you have come to learn, this world will no longer be necessary. This physical universe which seems so permanent to you will dissolve into nothingness. For once you are awake, it will serve no purpose. That time is coming, yet there is no rush.

Don't push the river. Don't try to hold it back. It won't do you any good. The Divine Mind is at work in your mind right here, right now. In this you must learn to trust.

The Need For Miracles

Miracles are demonstrations of the Divine Mind in action within your mind and experience. Miracles are needed as teaching devices, just as they were two thousand years ago. Every Miracle is a demonstration of the fact that love is stronger than fear.

Do not underestimate the degree to which your world is created out of fear. Look around you. Look at your own thoughts. Is there any place where fear does not have a foothold?

I don't ask you to do this to depress you. I would just have you be realistic. See things as they are in your world. Take an inventory of your own thoughts. You cannot come to love unless you realize how much of your thinking is fear-based.

Bringing awareness to your fearful thoughts introduces the possibility of an alternative. But please do not try to replace negative, fearful thoughts with positive, loving thoughts. This just sets up conflict in your mind. Instead, let awareness work. Simply be aware of your fear and feel it.

Then, when you have felt it fully, simply say: "I am ready to move through my fear now, Father.

Please help me." And be willing to receive the help you asked for. Your request will not be turned down, I assure you.

When you ask for help, you acknowledge that there is a power that is greater than your fear. You also indicate your desire to work with that power to move out of fear and conflict in your life.

There is one more suggestion I would make. When you ask for help, recognize that you are asking that your thoughts be changed. So affirm this: "Father, I am willing to change my mind about this situation. Please help me see this, not through the eyes of fear, but as You see it. Help me see this with equal love for myself and all others."

This, my brother, is a powerful prayer. Stay with it. Rest in its strength and its peace. And let God answer you in every word, every gesture and every action. You cannot experience the Miracle unless you are willing to receive it.

To experience the Miracle, the following factors must be present:

1. You must know that you need it.
2. You must ask for it sincerely.
3. You must be willing to receive it.

When all three factors are present, the Miracle will manifest.

Unfortunately, even if the Miracle has manifested in your life, you may not know it. Why is this?

Because you have a preconception of what the Miracle is supposed to look like. So even though it is sitting right next to you, you might not recognize it.

What good is a Miracle if you can't find it? If you would accept the Miracle into your heart, please understand that it might not look like you thought it would. Be open to its presence in your life, and allow it to reveal itself to you.

Some of you may ask: "Why doesn't God give me the Miracle I ask for?" That is because the Miracle you ask for may not free you from your fear. Therefore, it is not miraculous, and your fear will just recreate the conditions that necessitated the demonstration you asked for.

Let God be the one to answer your prayer. Do not try to tell Him what you need. He knows better than you do. Trust in that. Open to His presence in your life. Be willing to learn from Him and of Him. In that willingness, fear will be dissolved. In that willingness, you will awaken to your true nature.

Using What Is There

Y ou do not have to reinvent the wheel in order to make a meaningful contribution in life. If you look around, you will see many avenues for self-expression. None of these are perfect. Some will require you to adapt. That is okay. It is good to be adaptable. It is good to understand that the same thing can be said and done in many ways.

If you are trying to find the perfect form — the perfect job, the perfect relationship — you will be continually frustrated. The world does not offer perfection in this respect. It simply offers you an opportunity to grow and to change, which is not hard if you are not attached to the form of your expression.

Use the form that is available to you at the time. Let go of your preconceptions. Each moment is new. Each situation asks something different from you.

The attachment to saying or doing something a particular way is time bound. Such attachments keep you chained to the past. They keep you fixed in a false identity. Every experience that comes your way will ask you if you are willing to let go, if you are willing to trust, if you are willing to step out of time.

If you are not attached to form, it is easy to step out of time. Your focus remains in the present, in the eternal now. Whatever occurs demands your total attention.

Yet how many of you are fully present in your experience? Most of you are busy judging your experience, finding fault with it, wishing that it looked as you expected it to look. In other words, you are holding onto your false identity. You are trying to make the present conform to the past.

Ask yourself honestly: are you looking for a steady, predictable life? Is this what you want? If so, you must realize that the world cannot offer you this. Everything in the world is in the process of change. Nothing is steady. Nothing is predictable. Nothing will give you anything other than temporary security. Thoughts come and go. Relationships begin and end. Bodies are born and pass away. This is all the world can offer you: impermanence, growth, change.

Permanence cannot be found at the level of form. All form is in essence a distortion of the original formlessness of the universe. What is all inclusive, all accepting, all loving cannot be limited to form. Love does not choose its beloved or the moment of its expression. Love extends to all at all times. Love is without conditions; that it to say it is "without form."

Does this mean that you cannot experience love in the world? Of course not! However, your experience of love will be diminished in direct proportion to your need to interpret or control it. Interpretation places conditions upon that which must be without conditions. When you establish conditions on love, you experience the conditions, not the love. You encounter the form, not the content.

Love expresses only through an open heart. Openheartedness is not a technique, but an emotional willingness that moves beyond the limits of conceptual definition. As each form changes, the heart opens without fear to its changing content.

To understand anything in the world, you must learn to look beyond the form to the creative intention. Tune into the intention behind someone's expression and you will see more clearly what that expression means for him. But look at the naked form alone and you will see only what it means to you.

"Looking beyond the form" is another way of saying "look beyond your own preconceptions." To see your brother as he really is, you must look beyond your judgments of him. If you would know him you must come close to him, open your heart, and ask him what he intends. That is the only gesture that will bring you knowledge of him.

When one's intentions change, the form that carries those intentions changes. If you are sensitive to your own intentions and those of others, you will be better prepared for changes in form.

Detachment from form comes from familiarity with others, not from estrangement. Distancing others does not bring detachment, but its opposite. Only when you let others into your heart do you become capable of releasing them.

Compassion and detachment go hand in hand. You cannot love someone and seek to control him. Only by wanting what is best for him do you offer your brother freedom. And if you do not offer him freedom, you do not offer him love.

The attachment to form comes from the most profound insecurity. You cannot fully understand it until you move beyond that attachment. Yet this movement is inevitable. It is written in the blueprint of life.

Every situation in your life provides you with an opportunity to gain greater intimacy and greater freedom. As you love more and more people more and more deeply, you become less attached to them individually. You become attached not to the specific person, but to the love that each one extends to you. This is a movement toward the experience of Divine Love which is beyond the body, indeed beyond form of any kind.

When I ask you to use whatever form is available to you in the present moment, I am asking you to become flexible and receptive. I am asking you to move to the level of intention. I am asking you to move into intimacy without trying to define or control. If you do this, you will never be limited by form or obsessed by it. You will be free to create spontaneously.

That is the best advice I can give to you. Stay in the present without expectations, without attachment to outcome. Do not complain about the form that is offered to you, or invest it with more importance than it has. Perfection is not available outside of you.

If you would find truth, look within. Look at your own intentions. Then you cannot possibly mistake those of another.

Opening to the Divine

Until you understand that everyone is good, it will be hard for you to find goodness in yourself or others. You are used to finding the good along with the bad. "This is good; that is bad." This is your judgment of yourself and your brother. It will never bring you peace.

Your brother is not good or bad, nor are you. Both of you are only good. There is no bad in you. You may believe that there is bad in you — indeed you may believe that there is little or no good in you — but this is a mistaken belief. As long as you hold this belief, you will beat yourself up or you will beat others up.

What do I mean when I say there is only good in you? Does this mean that you are incapable of a negative thought or gesture? Certainly not, or you would not be where you are. Your world is a composite of negative thoughts and gestures, mixed in with positive ones. Yours is a shadowy world, a world of darkness and light commingled.

Yet this entire world you experience is made up only of thoughts. If you could eliminate negative thinking from your mind, you would live in a very different type of world.

In a world where there are only "good" thoughts, comparison is impossible. Without comparison there is no interpretation, so there can be no failure, punishment, sacrifice or suffering. Can you imagine such a shining, guiltless world? It may seem strange to you that such a world can exist, yet it is no harder to create than the world you inhabit!

You can begin to create this new world by understanding that there is no bad, but only good in you and in your brother. It is fear of the bad that makes "the bad" seem real. All negativity arises from fear. The very concept "bad" is a fear thought.

So beside your goodness, which is your birthright, what else is there? There is the doubt that you are not good. There is fear.

Your life is made up of goodness assaulted by doubt and fear. How many times during the course of a day do doubt and fear challenge your perception of your goodness? How many times do they challenge your perception of your brother's goodness?

Once you know that doubt and fear are constantly operating in your experience, you can consciously acknowledge them. Then, they simply become part of the dance of consciousness. "Oh, yes, I know I am good. But then what if I'm not?" This dance happens in the mind. Back and forth the dialogue goes. But gradually it loses its tone of condemnation. Gradually, as the fear is embraced, it slips away.

Conflict is erased from the mind that recognizes

its own goodness. And having recognized its own goodness, it cannot maintain it except by extending it to others. If you see another as bad, you have allowed doubt and fear back into your mind.

That which is divine is free of duality or conflict of any kind. You open to divinity when you see your good and that of your brother as one and the same. Divinity is always shared. It is never exclusive.

All exclusivity is the creation of fear. All judgment is the creation of fear.

Only when you reject the bad and accept the good will you cast fear out of your heart. Not one of God's children can be bad. At worst he is hurt. At worst he attacks others and blames them for his pain. But he is not bad.

Yes, your compassion must go this deep. There is no human being who does not deserve your forgiveness. There is no human being who does not deserve your love.

You can make your conditions and excuses, but they do not fool me. I have told you the truth. It is not in your interest to corrupt it.

If it is hard for you to forgive and to love someone, then say so. Do not condemn him in order to justify your own weakness. When you are in fear, tell the truth. Truth always brings sanity.

Only one who is in fear judges another. Are you beyond the grip of fear? If not, then recognize your fear. If you recognize your fear, you will not judge others. For you will come to see that fear always distorts your perception.

Recognize your fear and be truthful with yourself and with others. Confess: "I am in fear now, so I cannot see rightly."

Give up the judgments you would make, for they are but a meaningless attack against one whose goodness you cannot see. Surrender those judgments to me. Tell the truth: "Jesus, I cannot see this brother rightly, for I judge him. Help me to drop my judgments and understand what fears his behavior brings up for me."

Every judgment you make on your brother states very specifically what you hate or cannot accept about yourself. You never hate another unless he reminds you of yourself.

That is why every attempt to justify anger, fear and judgment fails miserably. It is merely an attempt to indict another for your own mistake. It lacks honesty. It lacks responsibility.

You have the means to end judgment totally, yet you would still justify it. Why? Because you cannot admit your mistake. You would prefer to suffer rather than to admit that you had made a mistake. You would rather pretend to be perfect than recognize that you are a learner here. What incomprehensible pride! How can I take the hand of one who, in spite of his pain, insists that he is perfect? I cannot help you if you do not let me.

To be mistaken is not so terrible a thing. It will

not deprive you of love and acceptance. You think that it will, but that is a fiction. What deprives you of love is your insistence on being right when you are not. That prevents correction from being made.

Please try to understand this. Being wrong does not mean being "bad" and being right does not mean being "good." Every one of you will be both right and wrong hundreds of times in a single day. I tell you that you cannot count the number of times you are right or wrong in the course of your journey here.

This world is a school and you have come here to learn. Learning means making mistakes and correcting them. Learning does not mean being right all the time. If you were right all the time, why would you need to come to school?

Be humble, my friend. You are here as a learner and must accept that this is so if you are to master your lessons. Lest you recognize that you have made a mistake, I cannot help you correct it.

But admit your mistake and correction will be there, along with forgiveness. That is the path I have set out for you.

Do not try to be perfect, my friend. That is an inappropriate goal. Only those who choose to suffer long and hard desire to be perfect. Desire instead to recognize every mistake you make that you might learn from it.

Perfection comes spontaneously and without effort only when you tell the truth, when you let go of your desire to impress others, when you surrender your false pride.

Those who ask for correction will receive it. This is not because they are better than others, but merely because they ask.

Do not judge those who are not ready to admit their mistakes. Simply admit your own and give the rest to God.

Share what your experience has been, but do not seek to thrust it upon others. For you do not know what others need and it is not up to you to know.

Remember the good in your brother. Remember the good in yourself. Let all fears and judgments dissolve where they arise. Admit your mistakes and be tolerant of the mistakes others make. That is what I ask of you.

It is simple, is it not? It is so simple you will keep forgetting it. But do not be discouraged. If your desire for peace is strong, you will eventually surrender to it. Once you have decided that this is what you want, you cannot fail to come home.

Learning to Listen

You are so busy reacting to what happens or does not happen in your life that you do not have time to savor your experience. You don't feel your joy or your pain, your anger or your grief. This is unfortunate.

You are wasting so much time looking for answers to your problems outside of yourself. If you just took the time to be with yourself, the answers would arise spontaneously.

Learn to be present with your experience. I'm not saying "try to figure it out." "Being with" is not an analytical activity. Indeed, recognize that you cannot figure your experience out. You can either be with it, or you can intellectualize it, which of course is an escape.

Every moment you are receiving suggestions which can help you steer the ship of your life back on course. But you cannot hear these suggestions if you don't take the time "to be" and "to listen."

Ironically, it is precisely at those times when you are most frantic trying to figure out and "fix" your problems that you most need to be quiet and listen. You may not realize that at first. But you can't help but notice that the more you try to figure things out the more confused they get.

Sooner or later you will give up trying "to make your life work" the way you think it should. And then perhaps you will wonder "why am I going through this transition time? Is there something in my focus that needs to change?" And you will learn to listen for the answer.

Usually, when you are on a collision course, the answer that you receive is something like: "slow down, look around. Maybe you are not really going where you think you're going."

That might not seem like such a great answer, but it is sufficient to help you take the next step. Slowing down and looking around is the beginning of correction.

As long as things are flowing smoothly in your life, you need not seek correction. But when the waters get turbulent, you would do well to pause and consider your course.

Just this much timely introspection would make a profound difference in your life. There are times when external reality simply closes down around you and the only appropriate place to go is within.

I am not asking you to meditate for two hours every day. Nor am I saying that regular meditation isn't helpful. I'm just saying that there are times in your life when you need to be quiet and listen. If you learn to honor those times, you will save yourself a lot of grief.

The more you learn to listen within, the more

you will begin to "be with" your experience as it happens. You will develop a partnership with your life, a willingness to participate, to feel and experience what comes along.

When you refuse to take time to be with your experience, it seems as if you are a victim of what happens in your life. That is a great self-deception. You have related to your experience as something you must conquer and control. And when your experience refuses to conform to your expectations, you feel that you are being unjustly punished. That is not what is happening. Instead, you are merely experiencing the negative effects of your need to control.

You are not open to your experience. You are not in constant relationship to it. You are not in dialogue with it. It is no wonder that you have a love & hate relationship with it. You love it when it goes your way and hate it when it does not. Yours is a black and white experience. Life is either totally blessing you or totally punishing you.

The truth is that life is neither blessing you or punishing you. It is working with you to help you awaken to the truth of who you are. Life is your teacher. It is giving you constant feedback, constant correction, but you do not choose to listen.

Choosing to listen means surrendering to your partnership with life. It means accepting the dance of thought, action and correction. It means experiencing all of this as a necessary but not unsavory part of the learning process.

Love Without Conditions

You have learned conditional love from people whose love for you was compromised by their own guilt and fear. These have been your role models. You need not be ashamed of this. You need only be aware of it as a fact.

From the time you were an infant, you were conditioned to value yourself only when people responded positively to you. You learned that your self worth was established externally. That was the fundamental error, which has perpetuated itself throughout your life.

Your parents' experience was no different from yours, nor was your childrens' experience. All of you need to heal from the same wounds. All trespasses/violations must be made conscious and the emotions attached to them must be released. This is the way that all wounded beings move from the experience of conditional love to the experience of love without conditions.

In the process of healing, you learn to give yourself the unconditional love you never received from your biological parents. And in this process you are "born again," and reparented, not by other authority figures, but by the Source of Love inside yourself.

Learning to give love to the wounded person within begins to reverse your belief that your self worth must be based on how others respond to you. Slowly you retrain yourself to value yourself as you are, here and now, without conditions. No one else can do this for you. People can assist and encourage, but no one can teach you how to love yourself. That is the work of each individual soul.

Each soul comes into physical experience intent to grapple with these issues of self-worth. However, very early on in the soul's sojourn here conditions are placed on its natural ability to love and include others in its experience.

Reversing these conditions is essential. If the soul leaves the physical world believing that it is the victim of its experience here, it will be drawn back again to unlearn that belief. However, if the soul awakens to the truth that its worth is not dependent on anything or anyone outside its mind or experience, it will establish itself in the Source of Love and awaken from the dream of abuse.

Awakening from abuse means rejecting the illusion that you are not lovable as you are. You demonstrate love by giving it unconditionally to yourself. And, as you do, you attract others into your life who are able to love you without conditions.

Your attempt to find love outside yourself always fails, because you cannot receive from another something you haven't given to yourself. When you withhold love from yourself, you attract others into your life who are doing the same thing.

The experience of unconditional love begins in your heart, not in someone else's. Don't make your ability to love yourself conditional on someone else's ability to love you. Don't place your faith in the conditions that surround love or in the form in which it presents itself. For these are impermanent and subject to the vicissitudes of every day life.

Real love does not change. It exists independently of the form through which it expresses. The Source of this eternal, omnipresent, formless Love is within you. This is where your faith must be placed, for this love is as certain as anything you will ever know. And once It is firmly established in your heart, you will never need to look for happiness outside of yourself.

People will come and go in your life. Some people will treat you well. Others will treat you unkindly. You will accept the love that its there and see lack of love for what it is, a cry for help from one who is hurting. You will encourage others to find the Source of love within as you did, knowing fully that you cannot fix their little problems. The tragedy of their lives can only be addressed by their willingness to look within their own hearts and minds.

One who loves without conditions places no limits on his freedom nor on anyone else's. He does not try to keep love, for to try to keep it is to lose it.

Love is a gift that must constantly be given as it is asked for in each situation. And the giver always knows when and to whom the gift is to be given.

There is nothing complicated about the act of love. It only becomes complicated when one starts to withhold love, and then it ceases to be love that one offers.

One who loves himself is not afraid to be alone. For being alone is an opportunity to love and accept himself ever more deeply. If his lover rejects him, does he feel unworthy? Does he pity himself and withdraw from the world, or bury himself in the search for a replacement? No. He simply continues breathing and extending his love at each step in his experience.

One who loves himself unconditionally does not love in degrees or with strings attached. He does not search for someone special to love. He loves everyone who stands before him. One person is no more worthy or unworthy of his love than another. This is the kind of love that is being born in you now, my brother and sister. This is the kind of love that I offer you and that I ask you to extend to others.

It is very clear. You cannot misunderstand what I am saying to you. Love can only exist between equals. Love can only exist between beings who have learned to love and value themselves internally.

Love takes no hostages. It makes no bargains. It is not compromised by fear. Indeed, where love is present, fear with all its myriad conditions cannot be.

I encourage you to be honest, my friend. What you know of love is not the kind of love I am describing. The kind of love I am describing is absolutely terrifying to you!

Why is this? Because the experience of Real Love ends your experience of the conditional world. When you experience It, you no longer feel separate from others. You lose every aspect of your identity that pushes others away. You open to a larger reality that you create with others through mutual trust. Judgment falls away and acceptance rules.

"I'm not afraid of that," you say. But consider it please. Be honest with yourself and with me. You ARE afraid of that, because it ends this dream and the only way your ego knows to end the dream is to die. So please recognize your fear of love, your fear of death, your fear of annihilation.

I have said "lest you die and be born again you shall not enter the kingdom of heaven." When I said this I was not talking about reincarnation. I was talking about the death of the ego, the death of all beliefs that separate you from others. I was talking about the end of judgment.

What dies is not you. What dies is everything that you thought you were. Every judgment you ever made about yourself or anyone else. That is what dies. And what is born again is full of light and clarity. It is the Christ that has eternal life, in you and in me.

I tell you, my brother and sister, your resurrection is at hand. And you are afraid of it! You cannot fool me. I see you trembling, on your knees, looking up at the cross where you will soon be lifted up to pay for your sinful thoughts and acts. Do not deny your fear or I will not be able to help you.

What dies on the cross is not you. You are not the body. You are not your fearful thoughts. All this can and will die. If not now, it will happen later. You cannot avoid the death of the ego. You cannot avoid the death of the body. But these are not necessarily the same. Do not make the mistake of believing that your ego dies when your body does, or that your body dies when your ego does.

Your ego dies when you no longer have use for it. Until then, it will not be taken from you. You can hold onto your ego almost forever, but you will not do this. For this is hell, and you will not want to live in hell forever. There will come a time when the pain will be overwhelming. There will come a time when you will call out to me "Jesus. Please help me. I am ready to let go." That time comes for every being, I assure you.

Until then, all you can do is walk though your fears. Acknowledge every fear you have and turn each one over to me. "Jesus, I am afraid to die ... Jesus, I am afraid of your love ... Jesus, I am afraid that God will abandon me." Let your fears come up and turn them over. That will quicken your awakening. That will take you directly to your core issues, to the fear beyond all your fears. Rest assured, when you come to that place, I will stand beside you.

Gentle brother and sister, I ask only for your trust. Give it to me and we shall walk together out of this place of shadows. I cannot protect you from facing your fears, but I can take your hand as you do so. Rest easy. The outcome of your journey is guaranteed. Where I am now, you shall also be. And then you will know with absolute certainty that Love is who you are. It has neither been born in you nor has it died in you. It is inseparable from you. It is your only Identity.

Opening the Door

To bring attention to any person or situation, you must be present to yourself, to the other person, and to the situation at hand. To be present, you cannot have an agenda of your own. If you have expectations of yourself, of another, or of the situation in general, you cannot be fully attentive in that moment. Your ability to be attentive depends on having an open mind, a mind that is free of judgment and free of expectation.

Equally important is having an open heart, which requires compassion for yourself and others, and forgiveness for the events of the past. Having an open heart means approaching others as equals and looking for common ground, opening to the intimacy and communion that are available there.

The door to love opens and closes as you open and close your mind and your heart. When the door closes, one needs to be patient and forgiving, or it may not open again.

One needs to feel not only the presence of love, but its absence as well. Feeling its absence, one learns to listen, and to soften in the heart. Feeling separate from others, one learns to look for the subtle judgments that are being made.

Every experience of separation or judgment is an opportunity to open to love's presence. Mentally, this involves moving away from fixed perceptions and their justifications. Emotionally, it means feeling the effect of separation: your own pain and the pain of another.

The shift from judgment to acceptance, from separation to empathy is the essence of healing. When you are unable to make this shift, you establish the conditions for dis-ease in the mind/body field.

All of you need to begin to learn to shift from dis-ease to ease, from constriction to openness, from distrust to trust. You need to learn to demonstrate peace by transforming "defensive" postures into a "receptive" ones, to demonstrate harmony in your relationships by transforming "exclusive" thoughts and actions to "inclusive" ones.

Being a healer or miracle worker means accepting your inherent capacity to be free of conflict, free of guilt, free of judgment or blame. If you accept this capacity in yourself, you will demonstrate miracles in your life just as I did.

I have told you many times that you can do this. Healing is not only possible, it is necessary. Every one of you is a healer of your own perceived injuries and injustices, and a witness to the power of the miracle. Healing is your only purpose here. The sooner you realize it the better.

Please remember that all authentic spiritual

practice begins with the cultivation of love for and acceptance of yourself. Don't try to love other people before you learn to love yourself. You won't be able to do it.

When someone comes into your life who pushes all your buttons, don't try to love that person. Just don't dump on him. Don't accuse him, blame him or make him an enemy. Simply acknowledge that he pushes your buttons and ask for time to be with your feelings.

When you are alone, remind yourself that what you are feeling belongs to you only. The other person has nothing to do with what you are feeling. Disengage from all thoughts that would make the other person responsible for what you are feeling.
Now be with your feeling and say to yourself: "what I am feeling shows me some aspect of myself which I am judging. I want to learn to accept all aspects of myself. I want to learn to bring love to all the wounded parts of me."

Now you have come to the place of genuine transformation. Now you are ready to bring love into your heart.

Practice this again and again and be patient with yourself. Don't try to heal your brothers and sisters and the world around you before you have learned to bring love into your own heart. That attempt leads to failure and more self-judgment.

Be compassionate with yourself. Take small steps. Begin healing your own thoughts and feelings.

Every time you heal a judgmental thought or feeling of separation, it is felt by every mind and heart in the universe. Your healing belongs not just to you, but to all beings.

When you come to peace, world peace becomes immanent. If you have a responsibility to others it is only this one: that you come to peace in your own heart and mind.

Some people think that such advice is selfish and irresponsible. They believe that they must save the world to find happiness. That is an error in perception. Unless they find happiness first, the world is doomed.

This may be hard for you to hear, but it is the truth. Unless you are happy now, you will never find happiness. So if you are not happy now, stop trying to find happiness in the future and bring your attention to the present moment. That is where your happiness is.

An open heart and an open mind are the door that opens to love's presence. Even when the door is closed, it bids you open it. Even when you are judging and feeling separate from another, love calls to you from within.

I have told you that, no matter how many times you have refused to enter the sanctuary, you have only to knock and the door will be opened to you. I have said to you "ask, and it shall be given you," but you refuse to believe me. You think that someone is counting your sins, your moments of indecision or recalcitrance, but it is not true. You are the only one counting.

I say to you, brother, "stop counting, stop making excuses, stop pretending that the door is locked. I am here at the threshold. Reach out and take my hand and we will open the door and walk through together."

I am the door to love without conditions. When you walk through, you too will be the door.

Relinquishing Effort

What happens in your life is neutral, neither positive nor negative. You decide whether it is positive or negative, spiritual or mundane.

Everything in your experience can be endowed with spiritual qualities by bringing your love, acceptance or forgiveness to it. Even a terminal illness, a rape or a murder can be transformed by the power of your love.

You think you understand the meaning of the events that occur in your life. Nothing could be further from the truth. You don't understand the meaning of anything that happens, because you impose your own meaning on it.

If you wish to understand the meaning of what happens in your life, stop giving it your own meaning. Let the situation be. Feel it fully. Allow it to teach you why it has come into your life.

If you want to come right to the center of it, ask "how does this situation help me learn to love more fully? What does it ask me to give that I am still withholding?" That question will bring you to the core issue, because it demonstrates your willingness to look at the situation as a gift, rather than a punishment.

When you give the situation your own meaning, you will always view it as a punishment of you or someone else. That is what your fear does to any event that happens in your life. Your fear condemns you and your sister. Don't be surprised when this happens. Indeed, expect it.

Don't try to live without fear. To try to live without fear is the most fearful proposition you can imagine. Just acknowledge the fear and move through to the other end of it. Don't try to live without condemning yourself or others. Just see the condemnation and move through it in forgiveness.

Just because there is a choice at hand does not mean that you should be the one to make it. Just see the choice and let your awareness move you through it.

There is nothing that you can do that will procure your salvation. In fact, everything that you do will simply keep you from finding what is already there. Salvation is already there. You are already saved. You do not have to buy your salvation from me, from your brother, or from some church or synagogue.

You practice forgiveness not to buy your salvation, but because the practice of forgiveness allows you to experience salvation right here, right now. You learn to accept what comes as a gift, not because it brings you brownie points with God, but because acceptance reminds you that there is nothing wrong now, nor was there ever anything wrong. You learn to recognize those moments when you begin to shut down and push people away because you know that it feels better to stay soft, receptive and open.

Your entire spirituality is lived in this moment only. It has nothing to do with anything you have ever thought or felt in the past. It is happening right now, with the circumstance that lies before you.

You experience darkness and scarcity only when you find fault with the situation you are presented with in the moment. When you see the situation and feel gratitude for it, you experience only bliss.

Do not try to move out of darkness. Do not try to move into bliss. The movement takes place of itself. Just be willing to move and let that willingness move you.

Most of what you try to do for yourself will not succeed because you do not know who you really are. Your self image is limited. You do not know or feel the extent of God's love for you. You think that somewhere along the line something in you got broken, or perhaps you are just missing some parts. But that isn't true. You have no missing or broken parts. All of your wholeness is fully present right now.

Many of you study prosperity consciousness, yet what you do does not seem to prosper. Why is this? Because you do not know your true worth. If you knew your truth worth, you would not feel that something was missing from your life. You would feel grateful for everything you have.

The truth is that every thought prospers. Each thought that you think adds its energy, positive or negative, to the situation at hand. Negative thoughts prosper as well as positive thoughts. Because you have a mixture of positive and negative thoughts, your external situation reflects both.

However, you won't be able to make your negative thoughts go away by focusing on positive ones. In fact, the more you focus on positive thoughts, the more power you give to your negative thoughts. You cannot escape this paradox.

That's why you can forget your affirmations. They are just hocus pocus. Stop trying to change your negative thoughts and just be aware of them. Be aware of the emotions attached to them. And let your awareness move you.

How will you learn to be supported by Divine law if you are always interfering in its workings. I tell you you cannot fix yourself. Your attempt to fix yourself just fractures your consciousness into smaller pieces.

It may appear that I am telling you two things which contradict one another, but that is not the case. I am telling you that your life has only the meaning you give it and that you can choose to give it a positive meaning or a negative one. And I am also telling you that any meaning you give it will be limited. Both statements are true.

When you watch your thoughts you become aware that part of you wants one result and another part of you wants another. You feel that you have to choose between these two parts and that brings pressure and conflict.

When your mind is in conflict, you do not move out of conflict by choosing between two opposing positions. That will just set up a more intense conflict.

You move out of conflict by accepting both positions. In other words you accept the positive thoughts and negative thoughts together, without making one "better" than the other. This is a loving act.

Love always transcends any kind of dualism. Love never chooses sides. It always accepts the validity of both sides.

You believe that you must choose between right and wrong. But are you or anyone capable of determining what is right and what is wrong? As soon as you think you know, you have lost the thread of truth.

So don't try to choose. You don't know what is truth and what is falsehood. Don't embrace one side and reject the other. Embrace both, or embrace neither. Be neutral and you will meet life on its own terms.

Lest you find this place of neutrality, you will continue to impose your own meaning on what happens in your life, and there will always be some aspect of scarcity or punishment in it, because you do not know your own worth.

Do you see what I am saying? Even if there were something about you that needed fixing — and

I am not suggesting that this is the case — you would not know how to do the fixing. If you are broken, how can you fix yourself? If you are divided or in conflict, how can you create wholeness? Only that which is not broken can experience its wholeness.

Understand, brother, that here in this moment, there is nothing wrong with you or with your life. Everything is as it should be. Right now, in this moment, you are completely loved.

Are you in pain or conflict? Okay. But that does not mean that you are _not_ completely loved. The idea that being in pain cuts you off from love is an idea you have imposed on the situation. In truth, nothing cuts you off from love, save your own beliefs. And that is why you are in pain in the first place. You are in pain because you think and feel that you have been cut off from love.

You invert the truth of the situation. You make cause an effect and effect a cause. That is your fear in action. Understand this so that you can see beyond it. Let your awareness deepen. See your whole ego drama for what it is.

Understand that you create your experience of the world through your own fear. But do not beat yourself because you do this. Accept what you see and let it shift of itself. When you see the world in its utter neutrality, you will understand that it exists only as a tool for your own learning.

I do not want to confuse you with concepts. But you must understand how your fear inverts the truth. It makes you a victim of the world, and that is not true. As a victim, you will never know your creative power or your identity in Love.

Don't play at being a victim. It is an empty game, a game of mirrors. The one who trespasses on you is just a reflection of your own lack of self worth. You created his presence in your mirror. Stand up, confess your hatred for yourself and let that other person go. Holding grievances against him will not help you. Punishing him will not make you feel better.

Let those who abuse you go free. Pray for them and bless them. Do not hold them to you with thoughts of retribution. But gently release them with words of love and encouragement. And know that as you release them, you release yourself.

I can preach to you about the power of forgiveness, but you will never know how great that power is until you experience it. The willingness to forgive yourself and release others from your judgment is the greatest power you can know while you live in this embodiment. The only power that is greater is the power of love itself. And without the gesture of forgiveness, which removes the veil of fear, the power of love remains unharnessed.

Yet take heart, my friend. Every time you forgive, you dissolve a condition you have placed on your own capacity to love. Every time you forgive, love is awakened in you more deeply and your capacity to extend that love is increased. That is the nature of the journey.   Be at peace with it and it cannot fail to bring you home.

Transparency

When you have nothing to hide, the light of your conscious attention is no longer compromised by secret shame. Lies no longer need to be upheld. Your relationships are not cluttered with hidden agendas. Simplicity and clarity rule in your life, for there is no deception.

Each one of you has this clarity available to you right now if you have the courage to communicate all that you think and feel without hesitation. That is your gesture of trust toward your brother and sister. That is your willingness to be visible and vulnerable.

If you have a fear and share it, that fear and the guilt beneath it no longer remain hidden. If you think a thought that condemns another, you can deny it, disguise it or project it onto someone else. Or you can bring it up for attention and healing. You can hide your attack thoughts or you can confess them.

The ritual of confession, like most rituals, has ceased to embody the purpose behind it. It has nothing to do with receiving absolution from another. It has everything to do with rejecting the density of deceit and bringing fear and guilt into conscious awareness.

The one who hears the confession is not a judge, but a witness. He or she does not have to wear robes or be in a position of authority. Any witness will do, so long as the witness understands that her role is not to judge or condemn, but merely to listen with compassion.

There is no one who does not make mistakes. Trespass one against another, with or without intention, is commonplace. To expect to end all trespass is foolishness. Only one who is not in touch with his human vulnerability would aspire to such a lofty and ungrounded goal. And how can one who cannot embrace his humanity come to accept his divinity?

Mistakes will be made and I urge you to be thankful for each mistake you make. Each error is a gift because it brings you to correction. Celebrate the opportunity to bring all manipulation and deceit to the surface. Be thankful for the invitation to reach into the dark places of your mind and bring the contents to the light of conscious inspection.

When you justify your mistakes, you hang onto them, forcing yourself to defend them over and over again. This takes a great deal of time and energy. Indeed, if you are not careful, it can become the dominant theme of your life.

Why not confess your errors so that you don't have to spend all your time defending them? Own your deceit so that it doesn't chain you to the limitations of the past. Let each trespass be openly acknowledged. If you think poorly of your brother, tell him so and ask him to forgive you. Do this not to raise him on a pedestal, but to keep yourself from falling into the bottomless pit of self-hatred and despair. It is the medicine you need to live without fear, dishonesty and guilt. Take this medicine, my friend. I have offered it to you before, and I offer it to you once again.

The density of this world is a result of your lack of courage to admit your mistakes. It is a result of the game of pretense you play with your sister. Do you really think it possible that you could be more moral or more correct than she is?

The best that you can do is to be more skillful at hiding your mistakes. This is a sad and self-defeating game. I ask you to stop playing it.

I ask you to trust your sister and know that she does not stand above you in judgment, but side by side, as your equal. She cannot condemn you without condemning herself.

Confess to yourself. Confess to your mate, your boss, even to the stranger on the street. Do not be concerned about what people think. You are transmitting a revolutionary teaching. Your confession gives others permission to look at their own mistakes with compassion.

A woman who admits her mistakes is a beacon of light to others. She has shed her cloak of darkness. Light shines through her, for her mind is transparent, a clear channel through which truth flows without effort.

Her brother and sister know immediately that

she can be trusted and they reach out to take her hand. Such a woman is a true priest. Having forgiven her own sins, she can extend that forgiveness to others. Her authority does not come from outside, but from within. She has been ordained by no authority of the world. Yet each person who comes to her recognizes her, trusts her, and confides in her.

This is the truth about confession. And any man or woman can be a priest. Do not believe in the lies that are offered up to you in my name. Use your common sense.

And do not be ashamed if you have turned away from religion because you could not accept these lies. I too would have turned away from a church that offers nothing but deception, exclusiveness, and guilt.

You are right to reject false teachings. But do not allow let your anger at the hypocrisy of worldy men in priestly robes take you away from your direct relationship with me. Forget everything you have been taught by others and consider the truth now in your own heart. That is where we must meet, not in some pretentious building that mocks my teaching and my life.

Now consider the truth, my friend. You cannot have secrets from me or from your brother and leave your suffering behind. To end suffering, you must end all forms of deceit in your life. And that can only be done by telling the truth, to yourself, to me, and to your brother.

What do you have to lose, except the density and confusion of the world? Would you keep your secrets and remain in the labyrinth or would you confess them and be free of the dark, twisting streets? The choice is yours.

But do not fool yourself. There is no salvation in secrecy or darkness. Salvation is offered openly to everyone in the light of truth. And in that light no shadows of shame or sin can remain.

Have the courage to admit your mistakes so that you can forgive them and release yourself from pain, struggle, and deceit. Confide in your brother that he may one day confide in you. Do not deny the truth or pretend that you have not heard it. For I have told it to you here in simple words that you can understand. The rest is up to you, for Truth is not embraced until it is put into practice in your life.

Each of you is one facet in the many faceted jewel of God's love and grace. Each one of you has in your own way a simple dignity of expression. The beauty of one facet does not interfere with the splendor of another, but adds to it in both breadth and intensity.

What makes one facet shine is available to all. The light that is in me is also in you. And I am no more beloved by God than you are. This, brother and sister, you must come to know in your own heart. No amount of teaching or preaching will cause you to believe it.

That is why I ask you to practice. Remove the impurities of judgment that block the clarity of your perception. Remove the obstacles of competition, envy, and greed which block the flow of love through your heart. Confess your fears, your feelings of inadequacy, your trespasses and your grievances. Bring the darkness of your secret thoughts and feelings into the light of conscious attention.

There is no mistake that cannot be corrected. There is no trespass that cannot be forgiven. That is my teaching. It is not just through my words that you can understand it. Everything I taught I also demonstrated in my life. How then can I ask less of you, my friend?

The Awakening Heart

Unconditional love comes naturally to you. It is your nature to feel compassion for yourself and others. It is natural for you to want to reach out and comfort a friend. It is natural for you to receive the love of those who care about you.

None of this takes any effort. None of this takes any learning.

Why then is your experience of unconditional love so rare? The answer may surprise you.

In the beginning you were one with God and shared in the omnipotent power of His love. Nothing was impossible for you. But then you began to wonder what would happen if you created apart from God. Since you had never done this before, you weren't too sure of yourself. Doubt came in and you wondered "What if something goes wrong?" This doubt was just separation anxiety, but it gave rise to many other fearful thoughts. Among these thoughts was the thought "If I make a mess of things, God might be mad at me and withdraw His love from me." And that thought was the clincher.

It didn't take long to go from that thought to the experience of feeling guilty and cut off from God's loving presence. Now this separation was artificial and self-imposed, but it felt real to you. You believed it.

And so all that you created after that was the result of the belief: "God doesn't love me. He's unhappy with me. I'm not worthy of His love."

And so in your own mind you "fell from grace." You went from sharing in the omnipotent power of God's love to being afraid of that love. Another way of saying that is that you became afraid of your own creative power, and hid it away where you couldn't see it. You stopped being a creator and became a victim. You stopped being a cause and became an effect. In other words, you turned reality inside out. You made love fearful.

When you are feeling separate, it's hard to remember what it was like before separation occurred. Yet that seems to be your peculiar dilemma.

And to find your way back to God, you must retrace your steps and realize that the "separation" was your choice, not His. You asked "What if I abused this power?" And then you proceeded to make a world in which your power was fearful. You did not stop and wait for God's answer to your doubt and fear.

Had you listened to His answer, you would have heard something like this: "You are loved without conditions. I will never withdraw My love from you. Remembering that you are loved, you can only act in a loving way."

Had you listened to God's answer, your dream of separation would have come to an end. For God's answer immediately challenges your assumption that you are not loved. This assumption is the original neurotic idea. All victimhood begins with this idea. You cannot think "bad" things or perform "bad" acts unless you believe that you are "unworthy of love." All attack proceeds from this one assumption.

Adam and Eve asked the same "What if?" question: "What if I ate of the apple and became as powerful as God?" They too gave their own fearful answer, felt shame and hid themselves from God. You are asking the same question right now. You are chewing the same apple. You too are playing hide and seek with God.

Indeed, it is the continual asking and answering of this question which keeps your experience of victimhood in place. In your self-created world, you are either a victim or a victimizer. As you explore these roles, you see that there is little difference between them. The victim needs the victimizer and vice versa.

The question of evil does not arise until one doubts one's own worthiness to give and receive love. That is your existential state. You doubt that you are lovable … you and everyone else in your world. Now comes the choice, the only choice that you need to make: are you going to answer the question "am I lovable" or are you going to wait to hear God's answer?

It is that simple. Are you going to let God correct your original faulty assumption, or are you going accept this assumption as truth and build your life on its foundation?

It's never too late to stop chewing on the apple. It's never too late to realize that your answer to your own fearful inquiry is unsatisfactory. It's never too late to turn to God and say: "God. My answer has filled my mind with fear. My answer has brought only pain and struggle into my life. It must be the wrong answer. Will you please help me find another one?"

You see, your spiritual life on earth does not begin until you ask that question. It does not matter what religion you are. It does not matter what your social or economic standing is. Each one of you will come to a point in your life when you are ready to challenge your own false beliefs and assumptions. And that is the beginning of your healing, and the restoration of your power and purpose.

The doubting of your own doubt, the negating of your own negativity is the turning point, the end of the descent into matter and the beginning of the ascent into heaven. It is the renewal of your partnership with God, the New Covenant.

You can't be a partner with God so long as you see yourself or anyone else as a hapless victim. The New Covenant asks you to recognize the Kingdom of God in your own heart. That is another way of saying that you reject the idea that God is separate from you. You reject the idea that you are unlovable or that your brother is unlovable. You reject the idea of evil as a idea created in fear. You reject the idea that God's power can be abused.

The New Covenant is the acceptance of God's answer to the question "What if?" It is the beginning of your own personal salvation and the beginning of human reception of the Kingdom of God on earth.

Once upon a time, you rejected your creative partnership with God. Now you are ready to re-claim it. Once upon a time you entertained the idea that you could be unlovable in God's eyes. Now you reclaim your eternal love communion with Him.

When you accept God back into your life, your whole experience of the world and all the beings in it changes. You are a father and a mother to every child who approaches you, a son or daughter to every elderly person. You are a friend to friend and friendless alike. And you are a lover to the one who remembers he is loved and to the one who has forgotten.

There is no place where your loving presence and testimony to God's love is not needed. All are crying out for your gentle words. All would drink from the cup that quenched your thirst.

The dream of unhappiness comes to an end when it is questioned and rejected. If you are ques-tioning your unhappiness, you are awakening to the unconditional love that lies in your heart. If you are not questioning your unhappiness, you are deepening your experience of it so that you can hit bottom. For, until you hit bottom, you are content with your own answers.

No one can force another to awaken. Each person experiences the futility of giving and receiving conditional love when he or she is ready. Each person clings to separation and control until the pain of it is unbearable. The pain threshold is different for each individual, but everyone crosses it in the end.

That is why I ask you not to preach to others, but merely to extend love to them. Those who are ready to receive it will follow you and ask your help. Those who are not ready will continue on their journey without interfering with yours.

A minister "ministers" to those in need. He extends love those who ask for it, silently or in words. He does not browbeat unbelievers with words or concepts promising some future salvation.

Salvation is now for those who would be saved. Do not judge the others for it is not for you to judge. Those who come later into the lap of God's love are not less worthy than those who come sooner.

In truth, it is not God who lifts you up. Nor is it me. You lift yourself up as you remember how lovable you are and accept your role in God's plan.

Accepting your omnipotence is impossible without your reconciliation with God. For all power comes from Him. You share in that as an equal partner, but you can never exercise that power apart from Him. Even in the "What if" dream, you could never separate yourself totally from His love. In that dream, you crossed the threshold of pain and chose to return. So it is with everyone.

The power of God's love cannot be abused. It can be rejected, denied, hidden. But all rejection, denial, and secret guilt have limits. Truth can be distorted but it can never be completely eradicated or denied. A tiny light always remains in the deepest darkness. And that light will always be found when the desire to find it arises.

You, my friend, are the hero of your own dream. You are the dreamer of the darkness and the one who brings the light. You are tempter and savior rolled in one. This you will come to know if you do not know it already.

In this self-created drama, your only argument is with God. It seems to be with your brother, but it is not. The tree of good and evil grows in your own mind. And it is in your own mind that you explore the questions of inequality and abuse.

There will come a time when your answer and God's answer will be one and the same. And then the tree of good and evil will transform into the tree of life, indivisible and whole. Love will no longer have an opposite, but will extend freely in all directions.

When someone approaches you who would place a condition on your love or his, you will say to him: "brother, I have dreamed that dream and I know its outcome. It leads only to suffering and death. It does not do justice to either of us. Let us question the assumptions that give birth to it together. I am confident that together we can find a better way."

If you ever wonder what your purpose is here on earth, please read the above paragraph again. Then you will remember that your purpose is merely to answer the call for love wherever you hear it. This is not difficult to do if you are willing. It requires no special abilities or talents. The hows and whys of love take care of themselves, as you walk through the door that opens before you.

I never said that you should walk through brick walls or even that you should walk on water. I merely pointed to the open door and asked you if you were ready to enter. And that is all that you need to ask your brother.

One who loves without conditions is never attached to the outcome. People come and go and you will never know the whys and wherefores. Some you think will easily pass through the gate, yet they will turn suddenly away. Others you are convinced will never come within sight of the gate, yet they will cross the threshold with unexpected grace.

Do not be concerned. It is none of your business who comes and who goes. The covenant is made in every heart and only God knows who is ready and who is not. Let us leave the knowing to Him and merely place ourselves in His service. Life goes much more smoothly when we do His will. And in our trust of Him our hearts are filled to the brim and overflow with love and acceptance.

Thus do we come to know that the supply of love is limitless. It has no beginning or end. All the limits of Earth are absorbed in the boundless love of Heaven as the Kingdom of God is established in our own hearts.

Eliminating Scarcity Thinking

Scarcity Thinking results from your perception that you are not worthy of love. If you do not feel worthy of love, you will project lack outside you. You will see the glass as half empty, rather than half full.

If you see the glass as half empty, do not be surprised if before too long there is nothing left in the glass. Lack is the result of negative perception. Of course, the same principle works in reverse.

See the glass as half full and it won't be long before it is filled to the brim. When you know that you are worthy of love, you tend to interpret the words and actions of others in a loving way. You do not easily take offense. If someone is rude to you, you consider the possibility that he or she may be having a bad day. You don't feel victimized or abused.

How you view life depends on whether you feel lovable or unlovable, worthy or unworthy. Either way, you will create an external situation which reinforces your opinion of yourself.

All preoccupation with supply comes from living in the past. Lack is simply the remembrance of old wounds. These are too easily projected into the future.

To end scarcity thinking you must forgive the past. Whatever it has been no longer matters. It no longer has effect, because you have released it.

Do you feel unfairly treated? If so, you will project lack into your life. Only one who feels unfairly treated will be unfairly treated.

To end scarcity thinking, start with the awareness that you feel unfairly treated. Realize that this comes from your deep sense of unworthiness. Understand that you do not feel lovable right now.

Don't try to change your thought. Don't repeat the affirmation "I am lovable right now," hoping that it will reverse your conditioning. Simply be aware "I'm not feeling lovable right now. I feel unworthy. I feel mistreated. I feel scared that the bad things that happened in the past are going to happen again."

Just be aware of how your heart has tensed and tightened. Be aware how you have emotionally shut down. And ask yourself if you feel more safe now than you did before?

Information came to you and you had a choice as to whether to see it as negative or positive. You chose to see the glass as half empty. You chose to be a victim.

That's okay. Don't be ashamed. There is no need to tense up any further. There is no need to beat yourself up. Just be aware of what you chose and how it made you feel. See it and let it go.

"I see the choice I made and I see that it made me unhappy. I do not want to be unhappy, so I will make a different choice. I will see the glass as half full."

If you can say these words with emotional integrity, you will release the past, release the wound. Try it. It works.

You have practiced hard being a victim and have learned that role well. Don't think invincibility comes without practice. Just see your choice of victimhood and be willing to release it. That will be enough.

Abundance thinking means you feel loved and worthy right now. Now you can say that you feel this way, but if the phone rings and you find out that you just lost a lot of money or that your wife is leaving you, how worthy do you feel? Is the glass half empty or half full?

Just acknowledging your own fear-based thinking goes a long way toward transforming it. Emotional honesty is essential for spiritual growth.

You can't force yourself to think positively, but you can acknowledge your negativity. Acknowledging your negativity is a loving act. It is a gesture of hope. It says: "I see what is happening and I know there is a better way. I know that I can make another choice."

Giving yourself another choice is the work of individual redemption. Forgiving the past and letting it go sets the stage for choosing differently.

No matter how many times you have made the same mistake, you have a fresh opportunity to forgive yourself.

Without forgiveness, it is impossible to move out of scarcity thinking. And to forgive, you must become aware of all the ways in which you are hurting. You must acknowledge the wound. Then you can forgive it.

Hidden wounds have hidden agendas that hold us hostage to the past. Deep wounds may require bandaging at first, but to complete the healing process they must be exposed to air and sunlight. Conscious awareness must be brought to all unconscious beliefs and assumptions.

Scarcity is an important teacher. Every perception of lack in your surroundings mirrors an inner feeling of unworthiness that must be brought into conscious awareness.

The experience of scarcity is not God punishing you. It is you showing yourself a belief that needs to be corrected.

You have the capacity to love yourself. And that capacity must be awakened in you for authentic spiritual growth to take place.

You learn to love yourself by seeing how you withhold love from yourself. And you often see how you withhold love from yourself by seeing how you withhold it from others.

Abundance comes into your life, not because you have learned to memorize some mumbo jumbo incantation, but because you have learned to bring love to the wounded aspects of your psyche. Love heals all perception of division and conflict and restores the original perception of wholeness, free of sin or guilt.

When you have seen yourself as you really are, you know that love cannot be taken away from you. Love belongs to you eternally ... formless but everpresent, unconditional yet responding easily to the conditions at hand.

Whenever news comes that seems bad, consider this. Would God give you a questionable gift? Do not be misled by the wrapping on the box, but open it with an open heart. And if you still do not understand the meaning of the gift, be still and wait. God does not give questionable gifts.

Often you will not know the meaning of the gift until the gift is put to work in your life. That can be frustrating, but it is inevitable.

The gifts of God do not feed your ego expectations. Their value is of a higher order. They help you open to your true nature and purpose here. Sometimes they seem to close a door and you don't understand why. Only when the right door opens do you understand why the wrong door was closed.

Yours is a partnership with the Divine Mind. Please do not try to make abundance your responsibility or God's alone. You need Him and He needs you. Be willing to look at your fears and your feelings of unworthiness and He will help you to see the divine spark that lives in you.

If you are willing to love yourself, you will open the channel through which God's love can reach you. Open the door to abundance within your own mind, and see the gifts of love reflected all around you. And please, do not judge the value of these gifts or the form that they take in your life. For the value is beyond question, and the form is too easily misunderstood.

Gratitude

You cannot mention abundance without also mentioning gratitude. Gratitude stems from worthiness and supports the experience of abundance. On the other hand, ungratefulness and resentment stem from unworthiness and reinforce the perception of scarcity.

Each is a closed circle.

To enter the circle of grace, you need to bring love to yourself or another. To enter the circle of fear, you need to withhold love from yourself or another.

When you stand inside of one circle, the reality of the other circle comes into question. This is why you often have the sense that there are two mutually exclusive worlds in your experience.

The grateful cannot imagine being unjustly treated. The resentful cannot imagine being loved by God. Which world would you inhabit? It is your choice.

In every moment you must decide to play the victim or remember that you cannot be unfairly treated. In the former case, you will resent the gift and see it as a punishment; in the latter, you will accept what comes your way knowing that it brings a blessing you cannot yet see.

Gratitude is the choice to see the love of God in all things. No being can be miserable who chooses thus. For the choice to appreciate leads to happiness as surely as the choice to depreciate leads to unhappiness and despair.

One gesture supports and uplifts. The other devalues and tears down.

How you choose to respond to life shapes your own continued perception. If you are living in despair, it is because you are choosing to depreciate the gifts that have been given you.

Each person who walks the earth reaps the results of the thoughts he has sown. And if he would change the nature of next year's harvest, he must change the thoughts he is thinking now.

Think a single grateful thought and you will see how true this simple statement is. The next time you are about to depreciate a gift that is given you, pause a moment and open your heart to receive that gift with gratitude. Then notice how your experience of the gift and relationship with the giver is transformed.

The next time you are poised to judge or condemn another, pause a moment and let that person into your heart. Bless where you would condemn. Judge not and be glad that you have not judged. Feel the release that comes to you when you let another be free of your narrow perceptions.

When I said to turn the other cheek, I instructed you to demonstrate to your brother that he could not hurt you. If he cannot hurt you, he cannot be guilty for his attack on you. And if he is not guilty, then he does not have to punish himself.

When you turn your cheek, you are not inviting your brother to hit you again. You are reminding him that there is no injury. You are telling him that you know that you cannot be unfairly treated. You are demonstrating to him your refusal to accept attack, for you know you are worthy and lovable in that moment. And knowing your worthiness, you cannot fail to see his.

The violations and trespasses of this world will end when you refuse to be a victim or a victimizer. Then you will step out of the circle of fear and all that you do and say will be filled with grace. This you will each experience.

Christ will be born in you as It was in me. But first you must set aside all unworthiness, all scarcity thinking, all resentment, all need to attack or defend. First, you must learn to turn the other cheek.

It seems that there are two worlds, but truly there is only one. Fear is but the lack of love. Scarcity is but the lack of abundance. Resentment is but the lack of gratitude.

Something cannot be lacking unless it was first present in abundance. Without presence, absence has no meaning.

This is like a game of hide and seek. Someone

has to hide first. Who will it be? Will it be you or me? Perhaps it will be the Creator Himself.

In truth, it matters not. When it is your turn, you will hide, and your brother will find you, as I found him. Every one gets a turn to hide and everyone eventually is found.

The world of duality emanates from wholeness and to wholeness returns. What is joined separates and comes together again. This is a simple dance. It need not be fearful.

I invite you to enter the dance without taking yourself too seriously. None of you are professional dancers. But every one of you is capable of learning the steps. When you step on someone else's toe, a simple "sorry" will do fine. You're all learning at the same time and mistakes are to be expected.

Freedom From Attachment

People who excel in the physical manifestation of their ideas learn to set realistic goals and to implement them in a flexible way, responding to the conditions at hand.

If you want to understand what flexibility means watch the behavior of a young sapling in the wind. Its trunk is thin and fragile, yet it has awesome strength and endurance. That is because it moves with the wind, not against it.

When conditions are right for something to happen, it will happen without great effort. When conditions are not right, even great effort will not succeed. Moving with the wind requires a sensitivity to the conditions at hand. There are times to rest and retreat, and times to move energetically forward.

Knowing when to move and when not to move is a matter of common sense and intuition. Abstract thinking by itself cannot lead to true perception. It needs to be combined with emotional sensitivity.

To see things accurately, you must understand your emotional investment in a situation, as well as its external appearance or behavior. Both inner and outer realities must be taken into account.

Some people say that the inner reality determines the outer reality. Others say that the outer determines the inner. Both are true. The chicken wouldn't be there without the egg or vice versa. Cause and effect are not linear and sequential. They manifest simultaneously. They are circular in nature. Not only does cause determine effect, but effect also determines cause.

The answer to the question "which came first, the chicken or the egg?" can only be neither or both. The chicken and the egg are simultaneous creations.

All either\or questions must be answered in the same way, or the answer will be false. Supreme Reality cannot be apprehended from a dualistic frame of reference. It includes both inner subjective reality and outer objective reality, as well as their mutual, spontaneous interplay. All opposites are contained within it.

Supreme Reality is the creation of total acceptance, total surrender, total all-inclusive love. There is nothing that is separate from it.

Even when trees are uprooted and swept away downstream, there is no tragedy. For there is no difference between the tree and the stream.

In contrast to the flow of Supreme Reality, there is Resistance, which gives birth to various conditions. Distinctions, comparisons and judgments arise and the natural flow is interrupted.

The nature of Supreme Reality is to say "Yes." It has a natural exuberance and enthusiasm. It would take all things with it. It is happiness personified, for it takes everyone and everything as itself.

Resistance always says "No." By nature it brings conflict and struggle. It would oppose everything and so it is unhappiness personified.

Where there is no resistance, there is no unhappiness. Unhappiness always resists some condition. It establishes itself on some interpretation for or against. The root of unhappiness is attachment.

Now I am not asking you to give up all your attachments. That, my friend, is not a realistic goal. I simply ask you to become aware of your attachments, your perceptions, your interpretations for or against. I simply ask you to notice how you have made your happiness conditional.

If you want to understand the unconditional, look at the tree moving in the wind. That is the best metaphor you will find. The tree has deep roots and wide branches. It is fixed below, flexible above. It is a symbol of strength and surrender.

You can develop the same strength of character by moving flexibly with all the situations in your life. Stand tall and be rooted in the moment. Know your needs, but allow them to be met as life knows how. Do not insist that your needs be met in a certain way. If you do, you will offer unnecessary resistance. The trunk of the tree snaps when it tries to stand against the wind.

Move in the wind. Your life is a dance. It is neither good nor bad. It is a movement, a continuum.

Your choice is a simple one. You can dance or not. Deciding not to dance will not remove you from the dancefloor. The dance will continue on around you.

The dance will go on and you are part of it. There is a simple dignity in this. I encourage you to enjoy the simple grace of being alive. If you are seeking a greater meaning in life, you will be disappointed. Beyond the dance, there is no meaning.

All conditions open of themselves to the unconditional. Simply be open and present, and you will fall into the arms of God. But resist even for a moment and you will get caught in a needless tangle of your own making.

Human beings cannot be free of conditional reality, because conditional reality is a creation of human consciousness. Stop trying to escape your own creations. Simply accept them, as the tree accepts the wind. Your dignity lies in becoming fully human, fully receptive to your own needs and those of others. Compassion comes not by cutting yourself off from the range of emotional experience, but by participating fully in it.

Some have said that this world is a painful place. That is absurd. This world is neither joyful nor painful, or you may say it is both at once. This world is a birthing place for the emotional and mental body. Physical birth and death simply facilitate the development of a thinking/feeling consciousness which is responsible for its own creations.

It is absurd to deny the importance of this birthing work. And it is equally absurd to glorify it. There is no human being who participates in the journey of birth who does not experience both joy and pain.

Are both necessary?

Absolutely. Without pain, the mother would not expel the baby from the birth canal. And without the joy of the newborn life, the pain would have no meaning.

But do not say "this is a place of pain, or this is a place of joy." Do not seek to make of your experience what it is not. Stay away from interpretations which would have you embrace only one end of the spectrum of life.

My experience here was no different than yours. I did not conquer pain. I surrendered to it. I did not overcome death, I went willingly through it. I did not glorify the body, nor did I condemn it. I did not call this world heaven or hell, but taught that both are of your own making.

I entered the dance of life as you have entered it, to grow in understanding and acceptance, to move from conditional love to the experience of love without conditions. There is nothing that you have felt or experienced, dear brother and sister, that I have not tasted. I know every desire and every fear, for I have lived through them all. And my release from them came through no special dispensation.

You see, I am no better dancer than you are. I

simply offered my willingness to participate and to learn, and that is all that I ask of you. Be willing. Participate. Touch and be touched. Feel everything. Open your arms to life and let your heart be touched. That is why you are here.

When the heart opens, it is filled with love. And its ability to give and receive is no longer based on anything external. It gives without thought of return, because giving is the greatest gift. And it receives, not for itself alone, but that others may experience the gift too.

The laws of this world no longer limit the man or woman whose heart is open. And so miracles happen, not through any special activity, but merely as an extension of love itself.

Miracles do not come from linear, sequential thinking. They cannot be planned. One cannot learn to perform them or to receive them. Miracles come spontaneously to the heart that has opened and the mind that has surrendered its need to control or to know.

For the Mind of God is Innocent and All-Giving. It cannot withhold its supply from you, for you are part of it. It knows you not as separate. Like a parent looking upon its only child, it looks upon you with steadfast love and affection.

"Reach out and receive these gifts," It calls to you. But you do not heed its call. In your frustration, you do not hear the Divine voice calling to you. As you look around at the conditions of your life and find fault with them, you are not aware that the unconditional love of God surrounds you.

Yet, no matter how far you may feel from God, you are but one thought away. And right now is the moment of your salvation.

Remember this, dear friend. Right now, in this moment, you are either listening to the voice of God or you are needlessly enmeshed in your own psychodrama. Right now, you are either happy or you are finding fault with the circumstances of your life. Let yourself be present to your thoughts and ask: "am I aware of God's unconditional love for me right now."

If the answer is "yes," you will feel the warmth of the Divine Presence in your heart. And if the answer is "no," your awareness will cause you to remember that Presence and draw it to you. This simple practice cannot fail. Try it and see for yourself.

As you learn to be open to the present moment, you will become increasingly aware of the Divine Presence in your mind and experience. Your personal purpose will unfold in this expanded consciousness, helping you to understand how you can best be of help to yourself and others.

Circumstances will come into being before your eyes. The appearance will often seem perplexing, but you will not judge. You will not find fault with yourself or with others. You will learn to surrender to the situation at hand, doing the best that you can and resting in the strength of your own surrender. More and more, you will entrust the outcome to God, and know that your gift is always acceptable as it is. Is is always enough.

Thus, the time of self-crucifixion will come to an end, and peace will return to your mind. Then you will see me as I really am, for then you will have given birth to the Christ within yourself. I await that moment with great joy and certainty. For that is the moment of truth. That is the end of all separation. That is the end of all suffering.

The Glory of God Within

God is not an abstraction, but a living presence, all-good, all giving, happy, whole, and free.

I know this is hard for you to imagine. Yet I ask you to stretch your mind. Let go of the limits you place on what is possible. God is beyond these limits, for He is without form. Being formless, He abides in all things. There is no place where His presence cannot be found.

God is neither male nor female, for he has no body and therefore no gender. God is often referred to as "He" because he is masculine in relationship to us. We are the womb in which his Spirit is carried, nurtured and brought forth.

But though we stand thus in relation to him, as the bride to the bridegroom, God does not conform to some masculine image. He is neither warrior, nor shaman, nor savior. He is not the wise man with white hair, nor is he the wise woman either. All such images are anthropomorphic.

God is a loving presence that combines all of the positive masculine and feminine qualities. He is nurturing and also protective. He is gentle and kind as well as strong and assertive.

God has the wisdom of the old sage and the innocence of the young child. He has the strength of the warrior, as well as the sensitivity of the young mother. He is all this and more.

He is beyond definition. He cannot be limited to the concepts we have about Him.

As a non limited presence, His Spirit moves through our minds and our experience. We draw our very Essence from this presence. It is what we are, although we are not often consciously aware of our Essence.

Spirit, or Divine Essence, is not born and it does not die. It exists before physical birth and after physical death. This Essence is not subject to the highs and lows of mental-emotional experience. It is a steady, loving presence, to which we return when we have stopped crucifying ourselves or attacking others.

The Divine Essence in you is not different from the Divine Essence in your brother or sister. It is a single essence, a single Spirit. Bodies seem to make you separate from one another, but Divine Essence unites you. Minds may disagree, judge and attack each other, but Divine Essence holds all minds in simple harmony.

When you identify with the body or with thoughts of separation, you forget your Essence. You forget who you are. You think you are separate from your brother. You think you are separate from God. You could not judge or attack otherwise.

When you remember your Essence, you are also remembering your Spiritual connection to all Beings. Attack is impossible when you remember who you are.

You cannot know the glory of God unless you appreciate the Divine Essence within you. This has nothing to do with your sex, your race, your economic standing, your nationality or your religion. It has nothing to do with who you think you are or who others think you are.

Divine Essence within you is wholly lovable and loving. When you are in touch with your Essence, you know that you are acceptable exactly as you are. You know that there is nothing about you that needs to be improved or fixed. To know your Essence requires that you discard your self-judgments and criticisms. It requires that you throw away all of your criticisms of your brother or sister.

The more you learn to rest in this state, the easier your life will be. That is why so many spiritual paths suggest meditation and prayer as regular practices. God-communion is good for the nerves. It is essential for your overall well-being, physically, emotionally and mentally.

I do not ask you to meditate or pray for an hour a day, although there is nothing wrong with this. I simply ask you to remember your Divine Essence for five minutes out of each hour, or for one thought out of every ten. Let your remembrance of God be continual, so that you do not get absorbed in the soap opera of your life. Nine thoughts may be about needing to fix yourself or someone else, but let the tenth thought be about that which does not need fixing. Let the tenth thought be about something which is totally acceptable, totally lovable.

This was the rhythm the Sabbath was to establish. For six days you could be absorbed in the drama of work and struggle, but on the seventh day you were to remember God. The seventh day was to be a day of rest, of turning inward.

Let the wisdom of the Sabbath be brought into your daily life. That way you will not forget for very long who you are or who your brother is. Enter into the ritual of remembering and your days and hours and minutes will be transformed.

When you eat, God will sit at your table. When you speak with your brother, God will remind you to say something encouraging to him. And when you forget all this and yell at your wife or your husband, God will reach out and touch you gently and say with good humor: "Welcome to the soap opera." And you will learn to laugh at yourself and not take your self-initiated drama so seriously.

This is all a game of remembering. Once you realize this, the meaning of ritual will change totally for you. And then you can choose a form of ritual that helps you remember. It doesn't matter what form that is. Fortunately, there are enough forms around that everyone can find something he feels comfortable with.

Be easy with the choice your brother makes, even if it differs substantially from your own. Know that what helps him remember can only help you. And do not argue about the differences in form, which are insubstantial.

Nothing frustrates me more than empty arguments about form. Words and beliefs that separate people should be put aside. If you wish to walk a path of Grace, overlook the differences you see, find what you can share with others and focus on that.

Truth comes in all shapes and sizes, but it remains one simple truth. You must learn to see the truth in every form, in each situation. That is what a man or woman of peace must do.

You are entering a time when the barriers of culture and religion will be transcended. People of different tongues will learn to understand one another. With tolerance for diversity will come the perception of Universal values which can be embraced by all. This is a time of great importance. Each one of you has a significant role to play in the dismantling of the barriers to peace.

Therefore I encourage you to find the place within where you are are whole and complete. From that place, you will celebrate and accept all people who come into your life. From that place of peace within, you will be a peacemaker among women and men. This is my teaching. Throughout time, this has always been my teaching.

Other Dimensions

Yours is not the only dimension of experience. There are many classrooms, each with its own unique curriculum.

In your classroom, the primary subject is equality. You are here to learn that all beings are equal regardless of their apparent circumstances. Men and women, black and while, Hindu or Catholic are all equal in their existential worth. All inequalities are of your own making and must be abolished. Many of you have been working on this curriculum for some time. I won't tell you how long! You have developed many ingenious ways to distort your true spiritual equality with other people. Some of you live in poverty conditions, while others have multiple estates. Some have too much food to eat; others do not have enough. Please understand that, had you already mastered the curriculum here, these conditions of inequality would not exist.

You are here, therefore, to overcome the deep-seated belief that some beings are more worthy than others. How do you accomplish this?

First, you must accept the truth of equality for yourself. If you feel superior or inferior to any other human being, you have not accepted the truth about your spiritual identity.

Second, you must accept the equality of others around you. Accepting their equality means that if you have more than them, you are willing to share it. And if you have less, you are willing to ask for their help.

You also are here to learn to respect everyone's right to decide for herself. If you decide for another or let her decide for you, you haven't accepted your mutual equality.

This trespassing one upon the other seems to give you license to make your brother responsible for the decisions you make or decline to make. But it is a false license. In time you will realize that you can hurt and help only one person, and that is yourself. Until you learn to take responsibility for the decisions you make and give your brother the space to do the same, you will not embrace the truth about yourself or about him.

This seems to be a very simple issue. Yet the practice of equality is a profound one. It can transform your world and allow you to graduate together with all of your brothers and sisters.

When you leave your body, you will continue learning in a non-physical classroom. Learning there will be accelerated, because there is no time or space there to modulate the creative effect of thought.

In your world, it takes time for thoughts to translate into visible effects. In non-physical dimensions, the translation process is automatic. For example, if you think "I would like to go visit my friend Bob," you are instantly transported into Bob's living room. Your journey took no time and you traveled through no space.

Some of you have experienced communication with beings in non-physical dimensions. Obviously, such communication takes place purely through thought. Inter-dimensional communication is difficult, but not impossible. With practice, your ability to reach beyond your limited space/time world will increase.

Since learning is accelerated in the non-physical classrooms, many beings who leave their bodies master the ability to control their thoughts. They are therefore confident that they can re-enter the physical environment and demonstrate their mastery. Yet of the millions who try, only a handful are successful in demonstrating mastery in the dense physical environment.

There is an easy way for you to understand this. Your science teaches you that when you leave the gravity of earth's magnetic field, you become practically weightless and capable of performing athletic feats you would be unable to perform on earth. Science also teaches you that as you leave the dense atmosphere of earth, the aging process slows down. Many of the physical laws which pertain to earth change as you leave earth's environment.

When you leave the body, a similar phenomenon

happens. You experience a creative freedom unknown on earth, except perhaps in the dream state, when your attention is drawn inward and your bodily processes slow down. The dream state provides a good metaphor for the expansion of consciousness that occurs when the body is left behind.

In your dreams, you create your reality quite recklessly. You kill and are killed, make love to all kinds of people, move through incredible danger and have miraculous escapes. Few of you would ever attempt in your waking state what you attempt in the dream state. Non-physical experience is even more dramatic than the dream state. The creative possibilities are endless.

Earth school then becomes an environment for testing the skills you develop in the non-physical classrooms attached to earth. You can't graduate from earth school until you have demonstrated your mastery of the curriculum. All beings know this, and so all are anxious to incarnate in physical bodies to demonstrate the fact that they have learned their lessons.

Why do they have so much trouble? Let us go back to the metaphor of gravity. An athlete in a zero gravity environment has no trouble jumping fifteen feet high. He can even fly through the air. But bring him to earth and he is pressed to jump seven or eight feet high. And he wouldn't seriously entertain the thought of flying.

The dense conditions of physical experience are difficult to master. It takes time to develop physically. You start in your mother's womb totally dependent on her. When you are born, you are physically helpless. You have to learn to feed yourself, to walk, talk, and manipulate your environment. Let's face it, for someone who has recently experienced a non-physical environment where the effects of thought are instantaneous, this is pure torture. In time, consciousness contracts, and moves to more fully inhabit the physical body, thus shutting off awareness of other dimensions with their creative possibilities.

Put simply, consciousness gets absorbed into the density of the physical environment. There it feels trapped and victimized. It does not remember its less limited state. It does not remember that it is not a body.

In a few rare cases, consciousness does not fully contract when it enters the physical classroom. These people inhabit bodies, yet still retain the memory of the non-physical dimension. They know that they are not limited to the body. They know that they are not the victim of other people's thoughts and actions. They know that they can create reality through the power of their thought.

These people are master spiritual teachers. I was one among many of such teachers who incarnated in the physical level to help my brothers and sisters remember their true non-physical identity. Without the presence of these teachers, the density of the earth plane environment would overshadow the collective consciousness and block out most of the connection to spiritual knowledge. There have been times in human history when the earth experience has been dark indeed. You yourself call one of these times "the dark ages." Another dark age closer to your experience was the first two thirds of the twentieth century.

The time that you now inhabit the physical classroom is a time of transition. Technologically, you have the ability to destroy the physical environment many times over. Yet there is more light available on the planet now than there has been in any other time in history.

If this is true, you may wonder why I have not joined you in this physical incarnation. Many of you expect me to come again in human form, but this will not be the case. My work here is almost over. And my physical presence with you now would only delay the transformation you are poised to make.

By now most of you should know the nature of this transformation. You are here to finally overcome your victimhood. You are here to accept your creative power to determine your own reality and to help your brother embrace his creative power. You are ready to do this en masse. And I am here to help you do it. Through your non-physical communion with me and other teachers, you will learn to let go of the conditions that reinforce your suffering, and you will awaken to your own Divinity.

I need the help of each one of you to fulfill my

mission here. It will be through you that my teaching is demonstrated in each moment. That is why the emphasis can no longer be on words, which separate people. The emphasis must shift to the active demonstration of the principles of love and forgiveness.

Your individual and collective attunement to non-physical reality is an essential step in the planetary transformation process. Were I to be present physically, the experience of the crucifixion would be repeated. If you look around, you will see that it is still a common occurrence for those who challenge the ideas of the status quo to be defamed, abused, and persecuted. The only way for this to be avoided is for you yourself to wake up.

Do not condemn your brother to death even though he opposes your most sacred beliefs. For to condemn him is to condemn me. Neither place him on a pedestal, even though you believe that he is impeccable. For no one is impeccable. No one lives without making mistakes.

I too, dear brother, have made many mistakes. I have forsaken my brother and my God and I have blamed both for abandoning me. Do not make me special. Do not make any of your brothers special. You are all learning the same lessons.

Learn to celebrate your equality with your brothers and sisters. For thereby you establish your equality with me. And when you regard me as an equal our communication will greatly improve.

Whenever you take your brother or sister into

your heart, you open the door to me as well. There is no brother or sister who is not dear to me. For I see into the soul of both the criminal and his victim. I see both calling for love and acceptance, and I will not refuse them. Do not be shocked that I ask the same of you, who are my hands, my feet, and my voice in the world.

Be patient and steadfast, my brother and sister. Our work will not be done until there are no more victimizers or victims. Our journey will not be over until we have accepted God's love for us and communicated that love to everyone in our experience. There are no exceptions to this. Everyone is to be embraced, as he is, so that he may let go of his fear and his need to retaliate against others.

To walk with me is to be a servant of God and man simultaneously. You serve man by showing him that God remembers him and cares about him. You bring him food and drink and solace in his suffering. You embrace him and allow him to lay his head on your shoulder. And you encourage him to weep. Because he feels abandoned by his parents, his children, his lovers, and by God. And as he weeps, you comfort him. For how long has it been since you too felt abandoned and shed gut wrenching tears of sorrow and regret?

That is the nature of the human experience. It is only appropriate that you should have compassion for your brother. For you share the same experience of suffering and you share the same release.

When the lessons of equality are learned on earth, the electro-magnetic field of the planet will change and earth will give birth to a new and more glorious curriculum. The seeds of this transformation have already been sowed. Your job is to water and nurture them.

The Tyranny of Agreement

The ego's notion of love is based on agreement. It cannot conceive of love being present when two people disagree. Yet unless you are free to agree or disagree with your brother in any given situation, you cannot love him. For example, if your brother insists to you that he is a victim of someone else's actions toward him, will you agree with him? Of course, you won't. Even if he begs you to support him in his delusion, you will say "Sorry, brother. I do not see it that way."

On the other hand, when your sister feels called to take a controversial stand and asks for your support, will you deny her? Perhaps supporting her will mean that you too will need to take a risk, but you will not withhold your blessing just because her decision is unpopular.

Need I remind you that commitment to the truth is not popular? Often it means saying "yes" when others would say "no," or saying "no" when others would say "yes."

Many of you cannot imagine that saying "no" can be a loving act. Yet it is very easy to say "no" in a loving way. If your child is putting his hand on a hot stove, you say "no" quickly and firmly. You do not want him to hurt himself. And then you put your arm around him and reassure him that you love him.

How many times does your brother come to you with his hand on the stove? You cannot support behavior that you know will be hurtful to another person. And you don't want your friends to support that kind of behavior in you.

A friend is one who is free to agree or disagree. A friend will speak to you truthfully. She may or may not perceive the situation accurately, but she is not afraid to tell you what she thinks. A friend tells the truth and then reminds you that you are free to make your own choice.

This is love in action. A friend loves you equally when he is saying yes or no. He does not withhold his advice, nor does he try to impose his opinion on you. A friend wishes to be helpful. He treats you with respect and dignity, and he tells you the truth.

You can't be a friend if you are not willing to tell the truth. This doesn't mean that you are right. Being right and being honest are not necessarily the same thing.

When you are honest, you are giving the best that you can give with the awareness that you have. That is all that can be expected of you. Whether your advice is right or wrong is immaterial.

But honesty alone is not enough. Honesty and humility must go hand in hand. Your humility says to your brother "this is the way that I see it. I may be right or I may be wrong. How do you see it? After all, you are the one who must make the choice."

A humble person understands appropriate boundaries. He never seeks to usurp another's right and responsibility to make her own choices.

Because you constantly seek agreement, you rarely experience love without conditions. Agreement is the ultimate condition and therefore the ultimate codependency or collusion. It says "if your ego and my ego agree, I'll support you."

When two egos agree, you should be wary. That is because it is the nature of the ego to separate, to divide, to conflict with other egos. So when two egos agree, you can be sure that they are joining together to oppose another ego. This is not genuine agreement, but a temporary alliance. As soon as the common enemy is conquered, the alliance ceases to serve a purpose, and each ego returns to its own agenda.

Looking for love in agreement is not a very wise move. It is bound to bring you disappointment. You would do much better to look for love through disagreement.

You will remember that I told you "love your enemy." I did not say this to be perverse or difficult. I said this for several important reasons. First, it is easy for you to love your friend. Most of the time your friend agrees with you and supports you. So it is not hard to love him.

But your enemy disagrees with you. He believes that you are wrong. He sees your weaknesses and would do his best to exploit them. If you have a blind spot, you can be sure he sees it. To put it simply, your enemy is not willing to give you the benefit of the doubt. He is therefore your very best teacher.

Your enemy reflects back to you everything that you do not like about yourself. He shows you exactly where your fears and insecurities lie. If you listen to what your enemy is saying to you, you will know exactly where you must make corrections in yourself. Only one who opposes you thus can be such an effective teacher.

Why do I say "love" your enemy. I say love your enemy because if you do not love him you won't value the gift he brings to you.

No one can go through life without both allies and opponents. A good ally is willing to oppose you. And a good opponent is the best ally.

When you learn to love your enemy, you demonstrate your willingness to look at all of the dark places within your mind. Your enemy is simply a mirror into which you look until gradually the angry face that you see smiles back at you.

To make peace with your enemies, you must learn to see through their eyes, as well as through your own. Then you will develop compassion and move beyond conflict.

Remember, you do not have to agree with your

enemies to make peace with them. But you must learn to love them.

Peace does not come through the agreement of egos, for it is impossible for egos to agree. Peace comes when love and mutual respect are present. When love is present, your enemy becomes like a friend who is not afraid to disagree with you. You do not cast him out of your heart just because he sees things differently from you. You listen carefully to what he has to say.

When you listen to your enemy the same way that you would listen to your friend, it is not your ego doing the listening. The Spirit inside of you is listening to the Spirit inside of him.

The cause of all human conflict is a simple one: each side dehumanizes the other. Each side sees the other as less worthy. As long as each side perceives the other this way, even the simplest details cannot be negotiated. But let each side bring to the other the attitude of respect and acceptance, and even difficult details will be resolved.

Miracles come from love. The solutions that come from loving minds are without limit. The willingness to love — to regard each other as equals — is the essence behind all miracle making.

Out of a diversity of perspectives comes the one perspective that honors everyone. Yet this perspective will not be available until everyone has been heard. Your job, my friends, is to give every person a fair hearing. This is the essence of democracy, which is not only a spiritual ideal, but a living, moving breathing process.

When the process breaks down, the ideal is corrupted. But when the process remains strong — as awkward and ungainly as it often seems — the ideal cannot fail to manifest.

A society that tolerates differences of perspective is a society that is based on the practical demonstration of love and equality. Those who seek agreement build totalitarian systems where individual freedoms are sacrificed and the whole never benefits from the wisdom of the parts. Such systems are doomed to failure.

It takes courage to disagree. It takes wisdom and foresight to maintain an environment of equality in which all perspectives can be considered. The path to truth has never been an easy one. It certainly has never been one based on expediency.

The expedient solution to conflict is to exterminate all those with whom you disagree. The goal here is not to love, or even to understand, but to destroy your enemies. That has been the prevailing value system on your planet throughout its history.

The democratic approach is a brave new experiment. It says "let all voices be heard." It welcomes diversity and has faith in the essential worth of individual human beings. It asks you to love, respect, and learn from your opponents. It assumes that the human heart and mind are deep and wide enough to contain all these perspectives. Indeed, it entrusts its entire success on your ability to consider different points of view and, when appropriate, change your mind.

Totalitarian and fundamentalist ideas play to your fears. They are always creating enemies and seeking to overcome them. They believe that there is one side that is good and another side that is evil.

They are oversimplified and dualistic in their perceptions of the world. But the path of compassion, which is the path I teach, challenges you to love and accept all beings as equals. It makes no exceptions, for it knows that to condemn one person is to condemn all. It is not an easy path, for it recognizes that there will be continual challenges to your commitment to equality. And each challenge must be met with the full depth of your commitment if you are to demonstrate the truth.

Many people use my name in vain. They attribute abusive, judgmental ideas to me, and use them to justify all manner of vile acts. That is why I must tell you clearly: do not use my name in vain. Do not use my name to judge any man or woman. I have never taken one brother's side against another's. Nor would I ever ask that of you.

I have asked you to come to peace within your own mind. And I have asked you to come to peace with all of your brothers and sisters. How can you distort this simple teaching?

If you have heard me in your heart, you will know that you cannot use these ideas to justify any judgment or attack on any human being. When you would judge another, look within and ask "would I judge myself in this way?" For any judgment against your sister is also a judgment against yourself. And any judgment against yourself is a judgment against me.

For I am not separate from you. As you treat yourself and your sister you also treat me. We are inseparable. Our destiny is bound together.

Understand, my friend, that you will not find love if you seek agreement. Love runs deeper than that. As you learn to love the one who opposes you, you will find the Source that goes beyond judgment or fear. In that Source we are all joined as equals, free to think and act in accordance with our guidance.

I support you in your freedom to choose, even when you make a different choice than I would make. For I trust you, my sister. I trust God's plan for your awakening. And I know that you can never make a mistake that will cut you off from God's love or from mine.

Crime and Punishment

I f thoughts could kill, how many of you would still be alive? I would remind you: the seeds of all actions are to be found in your thoughts. "If you think, I can't stand so and so," you are attacking him.

What begins as thought quickly becomes speech. If you slander this person in front of others or plot behind his back, you are attacking him.

What becomes speech quickly becomes action. If your words inflame others who support you in your attack, you may feel justified when you beat this man or even kill him.

Society says: "only the physical action is reprehensible. Verbal attacks are unfortunate, but inevitable. And, no one would be foolish enough to try to hold another accountable for his thoughts."

And so you are outraged by the act of murder, but the thought of murder is acceptable. You have all had it. You are outraged by the act of rape or sexual abuse, yet you are not greatly disturbed by the thought of it.

I ask you to remember that everything that you think about, say or do to another person reflects back to you what you think about yourself. A negative thought about someone else demonstrates how you see yourself. Gossip about another or verbal abuse indicate your own feelings of shame and emotional rejection. And physical violence toward another indicates your own suicidal impulse.

This is no mystery. Only one who is hurting strikes out against others. And I ask you, how many of you are not hurting? How many of you are not striking out in little ways against others?

The difference between you and the one who rapes and murders is not as big as you think. I do not say this to make you feel bad. I say this to help you wake up to your responsibility to your brother.

If you can forgive yourself for having thoughts of revenge, why can't you forgive the man or woman who acts with vengeance? This person merely acts out what you have thought about.

I am not justifying the act of vengeance. I cannot justify any attack, and I am not suggesting that you do. I am simply asking you why do you cast this brother out of your heart? He is perhaps even more desperate for love and forgiveness than you are. Would you withhold it from him?

Your brother has been wounded deeply. He has grown up without a father. He has been addicted to drugs since he was nine years old. And he has lived in a project where he has never felt safe. Do you not feel some compassion for the wounded boy in the man who commits the crime?

If you were to step into his shoes, would you do that much better? Be honest, my friend. And in that honesty, you will find compassion, if not for the man, for the boy who became the man.

And I will tell you right now it is not the man who pushes the trigger, but the boy. It is the one who is overwhelmed and scared. It is the little one who does not feel loved and accepted. It is the wounded boy who strikes out, not the man.

My friends, there is no man. There is only the boy. Do not let your sight be distorted by the angry, disdainful face of the man. Beneath that hard exterior is overwhelming pain and self judgment. Beneath the mask of mismanaged manhood and vicious anger is the boy who does not believe he is lovable.

If you cannot embrace the boy in him, how can you embrace the boy or the girl in yourself? For his fear and yours are not so different.

Let us first take away your mask of moral superiority. And then let the boy or girl in you look out at the boy in him. That is where love and acceptance begin. That is where forgiveness has its roots.

Criminals are just one group of untouchables in your society. You do not want to look at their lives. You do not want to hear about their pain. You want to put them away where you do not have to deal with them. You do the same with the elderly, the mentally ill, the homeless, and so forth.

You see, my friend, you do not want the responsibility to love your brother. Yet without loving him, you cannot learn to love and accept yourself. Your brother is the key to your salvation. He always was and always will be.

Just as the individual denies and represses the negative tendencies he does not want to accept in himself, society denies and institutionalizes the problems it does not want to face. Both the individual and collective unconscious are filled with unspeakable wounds. Behavior at both levels is driven by the unacknowledged pain, guilt and fear embedded in these wounds.

Forgiveness brings a searchlight into these dark, secret places in self and society. It says to your own guilt and fear "come out and be seen. I need to understand you." And it says to the criminal "come out, meet the victims of your crime, make amends, begin the process of healing."

Acknowledging the wound is always the first step in the healing process. If you are not willing to face the fear behind the wound, individually and collectively, the healing process cannot begin.

It is hard for you to look at your own repressed pain. It is hard for society to look at the pain of its outcasts. But this must be done.

Everybody lives in a prison of reactivity until the wound is made conscious. It is not just the criminal who is behind bars. The men and women who put him there live behind different bars. If you don't bring your unconscious material into awareness it will express on its own distorted terms. If you don't work intentionally with the criminal to help him come to love and accept himself, he will re-enter society with the same anger and vindictiveness.

Building more prisons or putting more police on the streets will not make your neighborhoods safer. These actions just exacerbate the situation by raising the level of fear.

If you want to improve these situations, bring the work of forgiveness into the prisons and the neighborhoods. Hire more teachers and counselors and social workers. Feed people, challenge them emotionally and mentally. Offer them experiences of safe emotional bonding. Provide them with opportunities for education and training. Give them hope. Give them acceptance. Give them love.

This is the work of a peacemaker. This is service. This is embracing your brother as yourself.

And, please remember, in giving to others, you will be giving to yourself. Nobody gives love without receiving it. Nobody gives a gift he does not simultaneously receive.

It is time that you stopped trying to punish the sinner in yourself and the criminal in your society. Punishment simply reinforces rejection. That is the opposite of what is needed. Feelings of rejection must be mitigated and alleviated. Judgment and attack must be brought into the light of conscious awareness. Guilt and fear must be seen for what they are.

The work of rehabilitation is a work of integration. The darkness must be brought to light. All that is unacceptable must be made acceptable so that we can look at it without fear. The seeds of action must be found in thought, and addressed there. You cannot change actions without changing thoughts.

If you make certain thoughts taboo, you will be afraid to look at them. This is not constructive. Be willing to look at the murderous thoughts in the psyche so that you don't have to bury them in the unconscious.

Help people take responsibility for the thoughts that they think and the effects of those thoughts. Personal power and authentic self esteem begin with the realization that you have a choice about what to think, what to say, and how to act.

Those who strike out at others feel that they have no choice. Those who know they have a choice do not strike out at others.

This is the key. Show a man the choices he has and he will not commit a crime. Crime is another form of self-punishment, unconsciously chosen to address unconscious guilt. The criminal commits a crime because he is still trying to punish himself. And society obliges him, by punishing him and reinforcing his guilt.

The only way out of this vicious cycle is for society to drop the agenda of ostracism and punishment and commit to healing. Every person in pain must be asked to help himself. He must be helped to consciously identify his unworthiness and guilt. And he must be assisted in transforming these negative emotions and beliefs about himself into positive ones.

The lepers of your society are no different than the lepers of my time. They bear everyone's wounds on their skin. They are bold witnesses to the pain you do not want to deal with. Society should be grateful to them, for they are wayshowers. They point to the path of healing all human beings must take.

Power and Mastery

C ooperation with the natural laws of earth is essential for survival. However, there are other non-physical laws or principles of mind that help to shape your experience here.

For example, the thought activity of mind is fueled by looking outward and engaging in the affairs of the world. When mind turns inward to look upon itself, thought slows down and eventually comes to rest. The observer and the observed become one.

The practice of self observation is a powerful one. It breaks down the barrier between subject and object, creating a new possibility for intimacy. Past and future surrender to the present moment, the eternal "now," wherein all creative potential lies.

Power exists as potential. As soon as it manifests outwardly, as force, it must overcome the resistance of its environment. It is therefore weakened. Power remains strongest when it is held in trust and not outwardly expressed.

When you act, you commit yourself to a specific course of action. Changing that course then becomes difficult, particularly when a certain momentum is achieved.

Therefore, before acting, mentally project the anticipated action into the situation and get feedback from the people involved. Let go of your expectations and listen carefully. Your ability to see beyond your ego-based perceptions will help you get important and helpful information.

The conceptual mind expects linear results from every action taken. Yet linear results are rare. As soon as a force meets a resistance, its course is altered. It moves up, down, or around the obstruction. Often, it is deflected from its original trajectory.

In spite of this, all your planning anticipates linear outcomes. It is no wonder that you are disappointed so often.

Since most decisions are ill-taken, they tend to be recycled. They are brought into circular orbit by guilt. Guilt is like a magnetic field that keeps each decision open to constant doubt and reinterpretation. Guilt brings all actions home, offering the same choice over and over in different situations.

Guiltless action can only be taken when you mentally project yourself into certain situations and anticipate the outcomes. A plan that anticipates resistance and objection will fare better than one that does not.

This sounds like an intellectual process, but it is anything but that. It is a highly intuitive process that requires genuine listening skills. Action does not happen before guidance has been sought.

Ill considered actions are rarely effective. They

err at both ends of the spectrum. At the one end, they are impulsive. At the other end, they are over-deliberate and lack spontaneity.

If I ask you what it will feel like to say something to your friend James, you can answer me in two very different ways. You can think of James and consider your past history with him and answer based on the past. Or you can sit down, close your eyes, think of James, make the statement to him, and see how he reacts. The latter method will give you much better results than the former method.

All the information you need in your life is obtainable in the present moment through a simple method of inquiry. Of course, this method only works if you can ask for information from a neutral standpoint. Your preference will falsely influence and distort the answer you receive. To prevent distortion, earnestly state before asking: "I place my preferences and prejudices aside and open myself to a free and truthful answer."

The cyclical nature of thought and action bring up continual lessons for you. Those lessons always underscore the gap between what you want and expect will happen and what appears to manifest in your life. You keep trying to escape this dilemma, but it never works out, because the dilemma itself is necessary for your learning.

It is inevitable that you will focus your attention on people and things outside of you. This is the world of "conditions." It cannot give you what you want. It can only reflect back to you what you don't want.

The search for happiness in the world is a grim one. The world cannot make you happy. The sooner you learn this, the easier your struggle will be.

If you look honestly at your experience, you will see that you spend most of your time "resisting" or trying to avoid certain situations. Of course, the more you try to avoid these situations, the more they come up in your life. That is because you can't learn anything through avoidance and denial.

Only when you face and begin to take responsibility for the situation before you in the present will you begin to address it meaningfully. Facing your fears is the first step in the process of undoing.

You think that you are here to accomplish many glamorous and important things, but that is just your ego calling out for recognition. You are here not to do anything, but to undo the false ideas and beliefs you have about yourself and others. Nobody else can do this for you. You accepted these ideas and you must be the one to reject them.

There is nothing glamorous about rejecting falsehood. Indeed, it is a very earthy and sober process.

Please spend some time looking at your goals. How many of these goals have to do with accomplishing something in the world? You will see that many of them do. Don't be ashamed. Just realize that your attention is directed outward. And please recognize that, even if it were possible, accomplishing all of these goals would not make you happy.

Happiness happens only in the present moment. If you are happy now, there is nothing else to accomplish. Indeed, if you become concerned about whether you will be happy tomorrow or even five minutes from now, you will forget to be happy now. All your scheming and dreaming takes you away from your present happiness.

Many of you have very important jobs serving others. Yet you are not happy right now in this moment. I must ask you: at what price would you serve others?

Do you really believe that you can bring happiness to another when you yourself are worried and stressed? Surely, you know that this is not possible.

I need to ask you, friend, are you willing to give up your 'important' goals for the sake of your present happiness? Do you have the courage to claim the present moment without knowing where it will lead?

All of the chaos and confusion in your mind and your experience can be transcended through your simple decision to be wholly present and attentive right now. That is the miraculous truth.

Would you be free of all conflict, suffering, self-doubt and judgment? If so, give up all your outer goals, worries, and preoccupations, and simply be aware of yourself in this moment.

There is nothing glamorous about the process of awakening. People who awaken do not become famous spiritual teachers. They do not build fancy organizations. They live for the most part unnoticed by all but a few students who recognize their freedom and authority.

Teachers who are valued by the world tend to teach at a very superficial level. For the world rewards tangible outcomes and effects, and spiritual accomplishments tend to be intangible.

One who masters the mind is not valued by society. He may be the most powerful being alive, but you will not find him in a position of power. In truth, even if such a position were offered to him, he would not take it. Such a person is not concerned with the manipulation of outer events.

For him there is only one question: "Are you happy right now." If the answer is "yes," then you are already in heaven. If the answer is "no," then he simply asks "why not?"

You may give him thirty pages of testimony as to why you are unhappy, but he will simply ask again "why not?" And sooner or later, you will realize that all your reasons for not being happy still do not answer his question. Because you have a choice to be happy right now, and there is nothing except your own stubborn need to wallow in the past that prevents you from making a different choice.

All the master can do is ask "Why not?" He cannot tell you what to do or what not to do, for the responsibility for both doing and undoing belongs to you. All the master can do is encourage you to take that responsibility here and now.

Teachers who tell you what to do or what not to do are betraying their spiritual immaturity. A wise teacher asks good questions, but she gives very little advice.

Not Withholding Love

Giving another the love he needs strengthens that love in you. Withholding that love from him diminishes your awareness of love's presence.

When your brother acts inappropriately and demands your attention, he turns you off and you turn away from him. After all, you know you cannot meet his demands.

Yet by turning away from your brother, you withhold love from him. And when you withhold love from him, you are also withholding love from yourself.

Your brother only wants your love, but he does not know how to ask for it. Indeed, he is confused about what love is. So he asks for money, or sex, or something else. He tries to manipulate you to get what he wants.

Of course, you don't want to be manipulated. You don't want to reinforce his inappropriate behavior by giving into his demands. But you don't want to reject him either. So what do you do?

You act in a loving way toward him. You give him the love that he really wants. You give whatever you can give freely. And you don't worry that you aren't meeting his demands.

In others words, you say "yes" to loving him and "no" to being manipulated. You say "no," but you do not cast him out of your heart. You do not judge him, or separate from him. You refuse to be a victim or a victimizer. You offer him love in response to his fearful thoughts.

You say: "No, friend, I cannot give you what you ask, but I will find a way to support you that affirms both of us. I will not reject you. I will not pretend that you are less worthy than me. Your need for love is as important as mine and I honor it."

This is how the lover talks to the beloved. He does not say "I will do anything you want." He says "I will find a way to honor us both." The lover is equal to the beloved. They are the mutual expression of love.

It is important that you understand this. Many of you believe that if you do not say "yes" to another's demands you are not acting in a loving way. That is not true. Never say yes to another's demands. That is not loving yourself. Please be gentle with yourself. Do not place another's needs before your own. Love has nothing to do with sacrifice.

Please understand this. Some of you believe that you must say "no" to everyone to protect yourself from their demands. That is not true. By saying "no" to everyone you just hold onto your fear of intimacy. Distancing others physically or psychologically is a fear tactic. It has nothing to do with love.

Please see how you reject others to try to keep yourself and how you reject yourself in order to try to keep others. Both gestures are a denial of authenticity and intimacy.

Only the authentic person — one who honors his own truth — is capable of intimacy with another. Only the compassionate person — one who honors the other person's truth — is capable of being himself fully.

You cannot receive if you do not give who you are away. And you cannot give if you do not receive others as they are.

Do not capitulate to each other's demands. Refuse to be manipulated. Say "no" when you feel trespassed upon, and then forgive the trespass. Do not hold onto the "no." Do not let the "no" to the person's behavior become a "no" to their call for love and support. Forgive the trespass, and be willing again to love and support.

Practice this and stay in the moment. Let your "no" to manipulation become a "yes" to love and support. Let your "yes" to love and support become a "no" to manipulation. Honor yourself and others equally. Do not attack or you will be the victim. Do not defend or you will be the one who attacks.

Let love replace all your grievances. If you feel attacked, say no to the attack, but do not attack back. If you attack others, realize it and make amends. Do not carry your guilt into the next attack. Correct the problem in the moment.

The more you give love, the more love you will attract. That is because you stay in the vibration of love by loving. You stay in the vibration of abundance by giving.

You must learn to say yes to people's need for love and support. The more you do this, the less their behavior toward you will be motivated by fear.

If you wish to dissolve violence, do not make the fearful more afraid. Communicate to them your love and support. Love redeems. Hatred condemns.

You will never realize the power of love until you begin to exercise it in your life. Do not cast your enemies out of your heart, but learn to accept them there, and they will cease to be your enemies.

All anyone wants is to be loved and accepted as she is. Give her that and she will not be afraid. Give her that, and she will have no need to attack you.

It is time you understood that what you withhold from your sister you withhold from yourself. For she is not separate from you. And only in recognizing her worthiness is your own confirmed.

Meditation
on Feeling Loved

When your brother attacks you, realize that he is not feeling loved. If he felt love, he would not attack you. Do not react to his attack. Find a way to remind him that he is loved.

Do this again and again.

Here is a simple walking meditation.

One day, when you are feeling cheerful, go out into your community and when you see someone who is sad or angry, find a simple way to remind him that he is loved. Give him a smile, a flower, a balloon, a sandwich or a cup of coffee. Sing him a song or recite a poem. Say: "This is just for you. Please have a nice day."

Another time, when you are feeling depressed, do the same thing. Do this again and again. You will be amazed at the results. There is nothing more ecstatic than reminding others and yourself that you are loved.

Remember, no one can give love if he does not feel loved. Therefore, you have only one responsibility: feel the love that is there in your heart. And help others to feel it too.

Can you imagine a world in which each

person understood that his only responsibility was to give and receive love? That world, my friend, is at your fingertips.

Wherever there is lack in your life, there is a need to bring love. Whenever you think you are not getting enough, there is some aspect of love and support you are withholding from another.

Don't withhold your love and support. Give it freely that you may receive the abundance of love that is your birthright.

Do this meditation when you are feeling loved and see what happens. Do it when you are feeling attacked and experience the results.

Experiment. Play with it. Do not be concerned about the form that this meditation may take. Just be willing to practice and the form will take care of itself.

The Illusion of Objective Reality

All "objective" reality is based on subjective agreement. Yet, explore this area of agreement rigorously, you will see that it is paper thin, like a flimsy membrane draped over the world that you perceive. Behind that membrane, nobody agrees on anything.

Events occur with a certain rhythm and grace. But then you step in and try to give them meaning, and the rhythm and grace are lost. As soon as you think you know what something means, you cease to be able to understand it.

Understanding something requires your appreciation and sympathy. Move with the situation for a while, and its meaning spontaneously comes to you. It is not an intellectual process.

The intellect makes a judgment and goes out and finds support for that judgment. The world is made up of those who accept that judgment and those who oppose it. In such a world, there cannot but be competition, struggle, and greed.

You do not ask what the world would be like if it were free of judgment. But that, my friend, is the only question worth asking.

Are you asking that question now? Are you asking "what would my life be like right now if I were not judging it?' Until you have separated external events from the judgments you have placed upon them, you cannot know what they mean.

If you would know "reality," you must take your judgments away from it and dwell with it simply and profoundly. This can be done with any situation in your life.

Have you just been diagnosed with cancer? Well then, be with the cancer. Recognize that everything that you think about the cancer — positive or negative — is merely an interpretation of it. You are deciding what it means.

Do not decide what something means. Just let it be and dwell with it, move with it, breathe with it. Be free of thoughts about it and you will begin to understand it. You may not be able to put your understanding in words, or perhaps you may. It does not matter. Insight will come.

The meaning or purpose of things dwells deeply within your own mind. To discover that meaning you must look into your own mind. Looking outside at so called "objective" events and trying to find the meaning there is waste of time. It cannot be found there.

Of course, the first thing you want to do is to consult others about your condition. Call up the experts. Get a first, second and third opinion.

Well, be honest. Are you more clear after the

third opinion than you were after the first? Did consulting the experts give you insight or peace of mind?

If so, you better watch out! Substituting their interpretation for your own will not help you understand what is happening.

If you want to go right to the heart of the matter, stay away from all interpretation and be with the situation. When people come to you saying "I have the answer," send them politely away. Their answer is just as toxic for you as your own judgment of the situation.

Admit "I do not know what this means, so I will give myself time to find out." I will trust the same intelligent force which brought this situation into my life to reveal its meaning to me."

This is the most loving action you can take. This action will free you and everyone around you from the compulsion to judge, interpret or rationalize the situation.

You do not have to push others away. Invite them to come and be with you. Let them hold your hand. Look into their faces. Be grateful for their simple concern. And let them know: "there is nothing here that needs to be fixed … There is just something moving more deeply in my life."

To be free of judgment and interpretation is the easiest thing to do. Yet you find it exceedingly difficult. That is because you have forgotten how to be.

Thus, the simplest thing in life becomes the

goal of the most complex systems of meditation. You will find all kinds of methods to teach you "how to be." But, as long as there is a method, you will be "doing."

I am telling you to drop all your methods. They are not necessary. Simply cease judging, interpreting, conceptualizing, speculating. Let all that is not "being" fall away. And then being will flower of itself. Then grace will unfold out of the seeming randomness of events. And you will understand the meaning and be glad that it is so.

There is no one who would shrink from his purpose here once it has been revealed to him. But it cannot reveal itself as long as he is trying to force his life open.

Be patient. Be gentle. All the joy and beauty of your life is at hand now. Your purpose is fully manifesting in this moment.

Do not look for meaning outside your own experience. Just trust what is and be with it. That is the most profound teaching I can give you. For, in this simple practice, all the barriers to truth will come down.

The Miracle:
Coming to the End of Doing

The more you are trying to do in your life the stronger your fear of death will be. For death is the end of doing. It is the end of thinking and reacting emotionally to the thoughts and actions of others. Death is the end of separation...the end of the body, the end of the conditioned mind.

Passing beyond the body, there is no mind that thinks, no mind that schemes or dreams or plans, yet communication is instantaneous. Why is this?

The nature of mind is unlimited. It does not conform to time or space. It goes beyond all boundaries.

You experience only that portion of the mind that you, individually and collectively, have limited to fit your experience. Yet other aspects of mind operate beyond your understanding or awareness.

Death represents the end of the subjective, separated mind. It represents the end of communication as you know it, for your experience of communication happens between two separate, private minds. This experience of communication is illusory, that is to say it is an extremely limited description of an experience which is without limits. Those who have come close to death know that there is a reality which is beyond the limits of perception in this world. In that world, communication is spontaneous and all-inclusive. In other words, there is no one who does not know what you are thinking, and this does not bother you, for you know what everyone else is thinking too.

Because there are no private thoughts, every limited thought is quickly corrected by a less limited one. Since your sense of self tends to be defined by thought, there is a sense that "self" is constantly expanding as thought itself expands beyond its limits.

The interesting thing is that right now, without struggle or self-conscious effort, you are in communion with unlimited being. Your body is bathed in light. Your heart is capable of receiving unconditional love and your mind is capable of apprehending truth directly. All this is possible if you will just be quiet and willing to experience it.

Once you leave the body, you will have no choice. You will be in the experience of it, ready or not. If you resist the experience, you will gravitate toward another limited body which offers you a developmental experience of truth. If you are ready for the experience of unconditional love, you will move through every fear you ever had and every limit you ever placed upon yourself to a place that is beyond fear or limits. This is the place you call Heaven.

Going to Heaven, ending the cycle of birth and death, entering Nirvana, transcending Karma, moving beyond the conditioned mind all mean the same thing. This is the ultimate destination in the journey of consciousness. Everyone will arrive. Everyone will finally achieve mastery.

All forms of spiritual practice merely exist to help you save time. They invite you to the experience of unconditional love and grace here and now. They invite you to stop doing, to stop thinking, to stop scheming and dreaming. They invite you into silent communion with your self. They invite you to see every brother's thoughts and actions toward you as a mirror of your own thoughts about yourself.

They simplify the warp and woof of life to a single thought, a single breath, a single action. They tell you that every event, every relationship, every gesture of heart or mind is a vehicle for God awareness.

Throw out all the dogma and empty ritual and you will come to the core spiritual experience, the essential invitation to worship. It is there in every tradition.

Indeed, it is there within your heart and your mind: the call to peace, to joy, to happiness. To answer this call is to enter the path. It does not matter what you call it. It does not matter how you express it. The way of giving will open before you. And as you give, so will you receive from others.

The path has its own simple beauty and its own mystery. It is never what you think it is. Yet it is never beyond your own ability to intuit the next step.

Authentic spirituality is not linear. It is not prescriptive. It cannot tell you "do this and do that, and such and such will happen."

Whatever is done must come from deep inside. It must be fresh, clear and centered in the heart. It must be done spontaneously.

If there is any residue from the past, if there is any fear, trust will be missing and the miracle will not occur. Every thought that is free of fear, every action that is free of the compulsion to "do," to "save" or to "heal" is miraculous in nature. It is free of the laws of time and space yet operates with spontaneous efficacy within them.

Why is this true? Because it is unrehearsed. Because it does not come from the conditioned mind. Because it is spontaneous and fully trusting. Such a thought or action is a living prayer. It cannot be anticipated or repeated. It is not a product of your learning. It is a result of your living communion with the unconditioned mind.

Deeply imbedded in your psyche is the call to awaken. It does not sound like the call that anyone else hears. If you are listening to others, you will not hear the call.

But once you hear it, you will recognize that others hear it too, in their own way. And you will be able to join with them in simple support. Blessing them, you bless yourself. Setting them free to travel their own path, you will set yourself free to travel yours.

There is no competition. There is no greed. For there is nothing to "get," nothing to "achieve." All is there for the taking that it might be given away. And in every gift that is given, be it yours or another's, is the miracle contained.

The Way of Forgiveness

I have chosen the way of forgiveness, because it alone undoes the lock of time upon the wound. When there is no time, there is no wound.

Let go of the past, and you will have no grievances. It is simple, is it not?

Time makes the wound seem real. It makes death seem real. It makes all the changes that happen in your life seem real. Yet none of these are real.

If you could be without time for a single instant — and I assure that you can — you would understand your salvation. In that timeless moment, nothing you have said or done means anything. In that moment, there is nothing to own: no past, no future, no identity. There is just the moment of pure being, of non-separateness, of non-judgment.

This is the moment you inhabit all the time without knowing it. Imagine that: you are already in heaven and do not know it!

You are in heaven, but heaven is not acceptable to you. Heaven does not support your ego, your schemes and your dreams. Heaven does not support your power struggles, your lessons, or even your forgiveness process.

There is no need for forgiveness in heaven. Why not?" you ask. Because no one in heaven is guilty! No one who abides in the present moment has committed a crime or a misthought.

Heaven does not support your soap opera of crime and punishment. It does not support your soap opera of sin and salvation. In heaven, there is nothing that needs to be fixed.

In this moment also, there is nothing that needs to be fixed. Remember this, and you are in the kingdom.

You think you get to go to heaven by "being good." Yet no two of you can agree on what it means to be "good." Is it any wonder that the road map to heaven is a rather crooked affair?

Some of you have a more enlightened attitude. You believe that it is okay if you made a mistake, but you have to be saved from your sin. You have to reject your old ways and understand that I died for your sins! That, my friends, is just plain hogwash.

Why, I ask you, would I die for your sins? I did not commit them! I guess you think I'm a magnanimous guy. I'm so "good" I can just soak up your sins and not be affected by them. Then we're all okay, right?

Yes, but are we? Now you believe your salvation depends on me. And what if I don't deliver? Will you crucify me again? Or perhaps take your own life? Is that the way you demonstrate that every-thing is all right?

I'm really saying something a bit different. Yes, everything is all right, not in some distant future or by some act of faith on your part. Everything is all right now, without your needing to fix it, and without my needing to fix it.

If you want to understand this, you need to practice the forgiveness process. Whenever you think that someone or something is wrong, forgive yourself for thinking that thought. Whenever you think you are wrong, forgive yourself for thinking that thought.

Say to yourself: "this seems to be wrong, but what do I know? I probably have something to look at here that I don't want to see. That's why I think it's wrong, because I don't want to look at it."

Be willing to look at the things you would con-demn. That is the fastest way to dismantle your guilt.

Whatever or whomever you think is wrong just shows you what you think is wrong with you. That is your guilt, brother. Better look at it, or it's going to keep running your life.

Stop trying to make illusions true. Stop trying to justify your judgments. That will just deepen your conviction that you are separate from others.

Be brave. Take a real risk. See that what both-ers you is just your guilt. Look at everything that bothers you and forgive yourself for taking it so seri-ously. Only a guilty person would take anything in your mad world so seriously.

You have only one person to forgive in your journey and that is yourself. You are the judge. You are the jury. And you are the prisoner. An unholy trinity, to be sure!

Loosen up, my friend. Everything you think you did to others is just a form of self-punishment. You are the one who must live with the guilt, not them.

The more guilty you feel, the more you will beat yourself up. Projecting your guilt onto someone else and beating him up only adds to the guilt that you carry. The only way out of this labyrinth of fear is to practice forgiveness.

Forgive everything that you think is wrong by forgiving yourself for being in judgment. Look at every judgment you make with compassion for yourself and the person you are judging. Do not justify your judgments and you will not make your illusions real.

In the present moment, fear, judgment, and expectation are overturned. Past and future are brought into the now. And so there is only this moment and the way you see it now. And if you see it fearfully, you look straight at your fear. And if you see it judgmentally, you look straight at your judgment. And as you forgive your fear and your judgment, they get out of the way. And you're not looking through a glass darkly. You're dwelling at ease with what is.

Forgiveness is the way because it unlocks the grip of time upon the wound! Where there is no time, there is no wound.

You are not guilty of any sin, my brother. But you believe that you are. And while you believe this, you will need forgiveness. It is the only way out of your self-imposed illusion.

Mistakenly, you believe that you can hurt another and that this other can hurt you. These are the thoughts that run your world. And so you have come here to see all the effects of your beliefs and to recognize, at last, that they are not true.

If a single one of you could be hurt, if your wholeness could be compromised or damaged by suffering or death, then your world would be beyond heaven's reach, and all your murderous thoughts would run rampant throughout eternity. Yours would be a dark and unredeemable world.

I know, at times, it seems as if this were true. But it is not true now, nor has it been true, even in the darkest of times. Your world, your life, your thoughts have never been beyond the reach of heaven, for heaven is here, my brother, and heaven is now.

You see what you choose to see, because all perception is a choice. And when you cease to impose your meanings on what you see, your spiritual eyes will open, and you will see a world free of judgment and shining in its endless beauty.

The shackles of earth will fall away, and you will be free to ascend to your place amongst the brightest stars. There you will look down on earth, as I do now, and you will say with compassion: "there

I walked too, when I was afraid, and learned to walk through all my fears. It is a holy place, a place where every enemy became a friend, and every friend a brother and a teacher. A HOLY LAND, where the dream of death and separation came to an end. I feel privileged to have taken the journey and happy to be home at last."

Then you will know that you did not have to take the journey to be saved. You could have stayed home without any taint on your innocence. But had you not taken the journey, you would not have known your innocence, as I know it, and as our Father/Mother does.

An angel who has not fallen from grace can never be a co-creator with God, for he or she is not capable of conscious creation. To create consciously you must understand your creation. And to understand your creation, you must join with them and experience their journey.

This you have done, my friend. And so welcome home. Your journey through sin and death has left you spotless and exuberant.

Hallelujah! Lucifer has been redeemed. The prodigal son has returned home. All the angels in heaven are rejoicing. But those who have taken the journey themselves are also shedding tears of joy.

The Death of the Ego

I t is the nature of the ego to divide and conquer. Where it cannot divide, it cannot conquer. Every thought either separates or unites. Thoughts that separate one idea from another or one person from another obscure your awareness of the unity. Thoughts that link one person to another or one idea to another reveal the unity.

Ideas can become opponents just as easily as the people who think them. You think that you can attack people's ideas without attacking them, but there aren't many people who won't feel personally attacked when you attack their ideas.

People identify with the thoughts that they think. If you want to communicate with people, find a way to acknowledge and include their ideas. Then, when you express your own ideas, it will be easier for others to acknowledge them.

People will never be able to be together peacefully until their ideas can dwell together without competition. To accept another person's idea, even when you don't agree with it, is to extend to him respect and trust.

Dwelling together in peace requires that you

see what links you to others, nor what separates you. If you see what links you, you will respect your differences. If you see what separates you, you will try to overcome those differences.

The attempt to overcome differences invariably fails. That is because differences are healthy. As long as they are respected, they do not interfere with the potential for intimacy and cordial relations between people.

Always give another the space to be different. Then you will not be avoiding intimacy with him.

If you feel that you need to become like him to be accepted by him or that he needs to become like you to be accepted by you, you are trying "to overcome" the differences.

Just let the differences be. You are acceptable as you are, and so is he. Peace remains in your heart and in his. Everything is fine.

Begin to see how much you try to change others to fit your image of how you think they should be. Be aware of how others try to change you. Feel the push and the pull. That is the world of the ego.

Ego is the most insecure thing in the universe. That is why it is always trying to take sides and bolster its position. It has no native confidence in itself and therefore no generosity of spirit.

It hates everything because it hates itself. All its pride is but a show. Take ego apart and you find an open wound.

Ego is the part of you that doesn't know that

you are loved. It can't give love, because it doesn't know it has love to give.

How do the unloved and unlovable find love? That is the cry of every soul in exile in the world.

Ego must be taught that it has love. This is a threatening proposition, for as soon as ego recognizes it has love, it ceases to be ego. Ego must die as ego to be reborn as love.

Now you know why most people resist enlightenment. The idea of waking up is scary to anyone who is still asleep. You keep thinking "When I wake up, I may not be there!"

That is why your fear of death and your fear of waking up are the same fear. The unlimited, universal Self is not born until the limited, temporal self dies.

So death will come, one way or the other. Either you will die, or you will wake up, which is a different kind of dying.

Once you are awake, dying is no big deal. You have no more prized identity to lose. Whether you stay in physical form or not isn't important. Either way, you need to be present.

Dying is one of the best ways to learn to be present. If you want to wake up quickly, try dying. When you are dying, you are aware of things in a way you never were before. You notice every breath, every nuance, every flower, every word or gesture of love.

Dying is like a crash course in waking up. Now

that doesn't mean that everyone who dies wakes up. It just means they've taken the course.

Those who graduate from the course are content to be wherever they are sent. If that means somewhere in a body, so be it. If that means assisting someone in a body, that's fine too.

It doesn't really matter where you go because you have nothing to prove. You are there simply to be helpful.

Disengaging from meaningless identity is an inevitable aspect of the path back home. The less you have to protect, the more help that you can be. And the more help you give, the more blissful your experience becomes.

While I would not go so far as to say "dying is fun," I would say that dying is "not fun" only because you are still hanging onto some shred of self-definition.

Your whole experience on earth is a process of learning to trust in yourself, in your brother, and in God. In the final moment of awakening, when trust blossoms fully, these three aspects of Self merge into one.

That moment cannot be described in words, but I assure you that you will experience it. And until you experience it, nothing will ever make complete sense to you.

The Gift

Forgiveness is a gift that was given to you for all time. It is not something that comes to you or can be taken away. It is there always, and it is the only gift you will ever need to move beyond the experience of pain and suffering.

Forgiveness works in this world, but it is not of the world. It is of Spirit and cannot forget its origin. No matter how many times the gift is received and given, it can never be exhausted. For every sin or perception of sin, forgiveness waits with the answer.

You do not understand the immensity of the gift, because you have not accepted it into all areas of your life. You have not accepted it in all situations. When you do, you will know that there is nowhere it cannot go. There is no situation in which the gift cannot be given and received.

Forgiveness is the only gift that asks nothing in return. And so it is the only gift that can be given and received without guilt.

The all encompassing love that lies beyond the door that forgiveness opens is incomprehensible to you now. Therefore, talking about it is not helpful. Be as you are. Stand before the door and knock. Be patient and committed. Be willing to look at every painful and unhelpful thought and let it go. Know that every thought releases or imprisons you and choose to be released.

When peace comes to your heart, the door will open. The veil will be lifted. Moses will enter the promised land. Until then, dwell where you are, in the heart of your practice.

God gave you one gift for your journey and one gift alone. He said: "My son, remember, you can change your mind at any time."

He did not say: "Do not leave, Son." He did not say "Son, you will be miserable until you return to Me." He just said: "Remember, you can change your mind at any time."

You can change your mind about every painful and unforgiving thought that you think. You can question each unhappy thought and think another thought that releases you and brings joy into your heart.

God did not say: "I will not let My Son make mistakes." He said: "I trust in your return and I give you a gift to see you home."

All your mistakes mean nothing to God. To him, you are but a child exploring your world and, through trial and error, learning the rules that govern it.

God did not make those rules. You made them when you made this playground. You forgot only one thing, and God gave that to you with his blessing. He said: "No matter where your journey takes you, son, remember, you can change your mind at any time."

With a single loving thought, He made temporal what you would make final. He made unreal what you would make real.

You created the ashes of death. He created the wings of the phoenix. To every unhappy thought you would think, God gave a single answer. "Remember, son, you can change your mind at any time."

Like Prometheus, you tried to steal the fire of the gods. But He did not punish you for this. He did not chain you to the rock where you would live throughout all eternity with vultures as your only playmates. He said: "take the sacred fire, Son, but be careful, and remember you can change your mind at any time."

Like Adam and Eve, you stood in the garden and became curious about good and evil. When he knew your desire for knowledge would not pass, he sent the sacred snake to you with an apple and invited you to eat. Contrary to popular opinion, He did not trick you into sin and then banish you from the garden. He just said: "Be careful, my Son. When you eat this fruit, your perception of the world will change. This garden may suddenly seem a dry desert where nothing grows at all. Your body with all its innocent grace and wholeness may seem to be separated into parts, some of which you accept and some of which you feel ashamed. Your mind, which now shares my every thought, may seem to think thoughts opposed to mine. Duality and feelings of separation may seem to enter your consciousness and experience. All this and more may arise from this tiny bite you would eat, but remember, Son, you can change your mind at any time."

Not only does God not condemn you for your mistakes, he is not concerned about them. He knows the child will burn itself with an open flame. He knows the apple will give indigestion. But he also knows the child will learn to keep the flame carefully and use it to warm himself and light his way. And he knows the body will adjust to the acidic taste and use the apple for nourishment.

He knows that your decision "to know" will bring you into dangerous situations, situations when you think your happiness depends on the way another treats you, situations in which you forget you are not a vulnerable organism in an arid and hostile land.

He knows that you will forget your origin, and that there will be times in which the Garden seems but a distant memory, whose very existence is questionable. He knows that there will be times in which you blame him for all of your troubles and forget that you were the one who chose "to know." But all this does not concern him. Because, before you left hell-bent into your journey of separation, he said: "just a minute, Son. It may be a long time before we meet again. Won't you please accept this simple gift from me, and keep it wherever you go in remembrance of me?"

Most of you do not remember answering "yes, Father." But I assure you that you did. And so the voice of God went with you as you went into exile. And it is still with you now.

So, when you feel forlorn and lost, when you forget that you chose this journey, remember "you can change your mind at any time." I am here to help you remember that.

This is not my gift, but God's gift to you. Because I received the gift from Him, I can give it to you. And if you receive it of me, you can give it to your brother.

But I caution you, do not be concerned with the identity of the giver. I am not important. I am not the gift, but the one who extends it, as indeed are you. Let us remember the origin of the gift so that we can give it and receive it freely.

Christ is the giver and receiver of God's gift. And Christ is born in you every time you give or receive the gift. It does not matter who offers the gift of forgiveness to you. It can be your child, your parent, your friend or your enemy. All that is important is that you receive it of him. And as you receive it, you become the Christ and so does he.

All who give or receive God's gift are the hosts to the Christchild. Each one of you is Joseph and Mary, welcoming God's child into the world. And each of you is that child, who receives the gift of limitless love from mother and father.

You must be careful which stories you believe

in. Much of what you think comes from God is fabricated from your own fears and anxieties. If you seek truth, better not consult some Bible, holy book or scripture written in the past. Instead, turn your attention to the truth that right now is being written in your heart.

God gave you the gift of forgiveness. This gift travels with you wherever you go. When you do not trust it, he sends His Son to you to remind you of the gift. And His Son tells you that you must give the gift if you would keep it.

Many beings of light have come as the Christ, bringing that simple reminder. All of us have the same purpose, for Christ is not a person, but a keeper of the flame, a giver of the gift, and a messenger of love. Light comes from him, because he has remembered light in the darkness of the world. Love comes from him, because he has received the gift and learned to give it unconditionally to all who would receive it.

What we have done, you too will do and more. For in your salvation is the salvation of every Son of God. You who see the Christ in your brothers will help them see It in you. And so the Light of truth will be lit in many hearts and the star will rise again in the sky above Bethlehem.

Many magi — men and women of open heart and mind — will gather together to witness the birth of God's Son on earth. And many others will oppose Him, not understanding that He is Them. All dreams

of crucifixion, sacrifice, and loss will array themselves in vain against the forces of love, and once
again love will triumph.

Christ will reach out and take the wounded
child in his arms and comfort him. And that child
will arise in the light of His love and push the stone
of death aside. All the exiles will return home to the
heart of God, the promised land. If you read this,
know that this will happen to you. And take heart,
for I am with you.

Together, let us give thanks to God for His gift
of love and forgiveness, for his eternal trust in us to
find our way back home. Father, we remember that
your voice is with us in every circumstance and we
rely on It to guide our thoughts and our footsteps.
Thanks to you, we are not alone. Thanks to you, we
have our brothers. You did not let us leave comfortless,
but gave us mighty companions to light our way.

In your name, we celebrate our journey here,
and pray without ceasing for the end of guilt, the
single cause of suffering. And toward that end, we
embrace the gift you gave us, the only gift that we
can receive or give without guilt. Thank you father
for the gift of forgiveness. We will use it wisely. We
will use it in every circumstance. With it, we will
bring Your light to all the dark places of our souls.

BENEDICTION

There is only One Son of God
and You are Him.

From Him, you receive.
To Him, you give.

When you look at yourself,
may you remember.

When you look at your brother,
may you also remember.

When you look away in fear,
remember only this:

Subject and Object,
Lover and Beloved,

are not two,
but one and the same.

What you give
and what you receive

are reflections
of each other.

*P*aul Ferrini is the author of numerous books which help us heal the emotional body and embrace a spirituality grounded in the real challenges of daily life. Paul's work is heart-centered and experiential, empowering us to move through our fear and shame and share who we are authentically wiith others. Paul Ferrini is the editor of *Miracles Magazine*, a publication devoted to telling Miracle Stories that offer hope and inspiration to all of us. Paul's "Joining Together" conferences, retreats and workshops have helped thousands of people deepen their practice of forgiveness and open their hearts to the Divine presence in themselves and others.

Heartways Press
"Integrating Spirituality into Daily Life"
Books by Paul Ferrini

• **Love Without Conditions:**
Reflections of the Christ Mind
An incredible book from Jesus calling us to awaken to our own Christhood. Rarely has any book conveyed the teachings of the master in such a simple but profound manner. This book will help you to bring your understanding from the head to the heart so that you can model the teachings of love and forgiveness in your daily life.192 pp. paper ISBN 1-879159-15-5 $12.00

• **The Wisdom of the Self**
This ground-breaking book explores our authentic experience and our journey to wholeness. "Your life is your spiritual path. Don't be quick to abandon it for promises of bigger and better experiences. You are getting exactly the experiences you need to grow. If your growth seems too slow or uneventful for you, it is because you have not fully embraced the situations and relationships at hand ... To know the Self is to allow everything, to embrace the totality of who we are, all that we think and feel, all of our fear, all of our love." 229 pp. paper ISBN 1-879159-14-7 $12.00

• **The Twelve Steps Of Forgiveness**
A practical manual for healing ourselves and our relationships. This book gives us a step by step process for moving through our fears, projections, judgments, and guilt so that we can take responsibility for creating the life we want. With great gentleness, we learn to embrace our lessons and to find equality with others. A must read for all in recovery and others seeking spiritual wholeness. 128 pp. paper ISBN 1-879159-10-4 $10.00

• The Circle of Atonement

This book explores a healing process in which we confront our deep-seated guilt and fear, bringing love and forgiveness to the wounded child within. By surrendering our judgments of self and others, we overcome feelings of separation and dismantle co-dependent patterns that restrict our self-expression and ability to give and receive love. 224 pp. paper ISBN 1-879159-06-6 $12.00

• The Bridge to Reality

A Heart-centered Approach to *A Course in Miracles* and the Process of Inner Healing. Sharing his experiences of spiritual awakening, Paul emphasizes self-acceptance and forgiveness as cornerstones of spiritual practice. Presented with beautiful photos, this book conveys the essence of *The Course* as it is lived in daily life. 192 pp. paper ISBN 1-879159-03-1 $12.00

• From Ego To Self

108 illustrated affirmations designed to offer you a new way of viewing conflict situations so that you can overcome negative thinking and bring more energy, faith and optimism into your life. 128 pp. paper ISBN 1-879159-01-5 $10.00

● **Virtues Of The Way**
A lyrical work of contemporary scripture reminiscent of the Tao Te Ching. Beautifully illustrated, this inspirational book will help you cultivate the spiritual values required to fulfill your creative purpose and live in harmony with others. 64 pp. paper ISBN 1-879159-02-3 $7.50

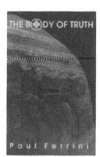

● **The Body Of Truth**
A crystal clear introduction to the universal teachings of love and forgiveness. This book traces all forms of suffering to negative attitudes and false beliefs, which we have the ability to transform. 64 pp. paper ISBN 1-879159-02-3 $7.50

● **Available Light**
Inspirational, passionate poems dealing with the work of inner integration, love and relationships, death and re-birth, loss and abundance, life purpose and the reality of spiritual vision.   128 pp. paper   ISBN 1-879159-05-8 $12.00

Guided Meditation Cassette Tapes
by Paul Ferrini

• **The Circle of Healing**
It's finally available. The meditation and healing tape that many of you have been requesting for months is now here. This gentle meditation opens the heart to love's presence and extends that love to all the beings in your experience. A powerful tape with inspirational piano accompaniment by Michael Gray.
ISBN #1-879159-08-2 $10.00

• **Healing the Wounded Child**
A potent healing tape that accesses old feelings of pain, fragmentation, self-judgment and separation and brings them into the light of conscious awareness and acceptance. Side two includes hauntingly beautiful "inner child" reading from The Bridge to Reality with piano accompaniment by Michael Gray.
ISBN #1-879159-11-2 $10.00

• **Forgiveness: Returning to the Original Blessing**
A Self Healing tape that helps us accept and learn from the mistakes we have made in the past. By letting go of our judgments and ending our ego-based search for perfection, we can bring our darkness to the light, dissolving anger, guilt, and shame. Piano accompaniment by Michael Gray.
ISBN #1-879159-12-0 $10.00

New from Heartways Press

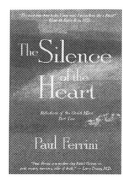

The Silence of the Heart
*Reflections of the
Christ Mind, Part Two*
240 pp. paper $14.95
ISBN: 1-879159-16-3

Miracles Magazine

Paul Ferrini is also the editor of *Miracles Magazine*, an international quarterly magazine published by the Miracles Community Network, a non-profit educational organization in South Deerfield, MA. *Miracles Magazine* is devoted to telling the stories of miracles that are happening in our lives. Each issue also includes in-depth articles and interviews with the leading healers of our times. For a complimentary copy, call 413-665-0555.

Heartways Press
Order Form

Name_____

Address_____

City _____State _____Zip _____

Phone _____

BOOKS

The Silence of the Heart ($14.95)   _____
Love Without Conditions ($12.00)   _____
The Wisdom of the Self ($12.00)   _____
The Twelve Steps of Forgiveness ($10.00)   _____
The Circle of Atonement ($12.00)   _____
The Bridge of Reality ($12.00)   _____
From Ego to Self ($10.00)   _____
Virtues of the Way ($7.50)   _____
The Body of Truth ($7.50)   _____
Available Light ($10.00)   _____

TAPES

The Circle of Healing ($10.00)   _____
Healing the Wounded Child ($10.00)   _____
Forgiveness: Returning to the Original Blessing ($10.00)   _____

SHIPPING

($2.00 for first item, $.50 each additional item.
Add additional $1.00 for first class postage.)   _____
MA residents please add 5% sales tax.   _____

                                    TOTAL $_____

Send Order To: Heartways Press
P. O. Box 181
South Deerfield, MA 01373
Tel: 413-665-0555

Please allow 1-2 weeks for delivery